TRANSFORMED BY THE WORD

A JOURNEY TO DEEPENING YOUR RELATIONSHIP WITH GOD

Mignon Valliere Walker

Transformed by the Word: A Journey to Deepening Your Relationship with God
by Mignon Valliere Walker
Published by Mignon Valliere Walker

Copyright © 2024 by Mignon Valliere Walker
All rights reserved. No material of this book may be reproduced or used in any form without prior written permission from the copyright owner.

The Scripture quotations taken from Holy Bible, New International Version ® NIV ®. Copyright © 1973, 1978, 1984, 2011 by Biblica, Inc.® Used with permission. All rights reserved worldwide.

For permissions contact: mignon.walker.1@gmail.com
Cover by Mignon Valliere Walker
ISBN: 978-0-9908789-7-1

Preface

Throughout my upbringing, I was taught God's word in some form or fashion. Let me give you some background. I was born and baptized Catholic. I grew up in a mixed bag of religions where parts of my family were Catholic, Jehovah's Witnesses, Apostolic, Pentecostal, and/or no religion at all. I was exposed to multiple religions and its practices. Depending on which part of my family I was visiting (sleepovers) meant I had to attend their church, learn and take part of those practices and traditions. I have to be honest, it didn't bother me at all because I knew that was a rule when/during sleepovers. I enjoyed going to church and learning God's Word. I never felt forced and it felt nice to be included. I really didn't focus on the means of each religion as I found myself more excited to be with my cousins. As I approached my pre-teen years, I decided to jump full into the religion I was baptized, Catholic. It wasn't until I got married in which I converted to Baptist. Because my upbringing was filled with multiple religions, I wanted to raise my family under one religion. And because my husband, the head of household, was Baptist, I/We chose Baptist. So, with all that being said, I was aware of God's Word. My means of reading the Bible was when I would crack it open during times of turmoil with self, job, in my household, my husband and I debated a scripture, and/or a few times to reference a scripture that was presented in church.

Throughout the course of my life, I've made several attempts to read the Bible cover to cover and failed each time. I also made every excuse known to man: I don't understand it, God speaks in riddles, I need a different Bible, I got off track of my reading schedule, I'll catch up my reading tomorrow, maybe I should buy some highlighters and color-code God's Word, maybe an African-American Bible is more suitable for my reading, how about I read just the summarized version of the Bible, I'll read the Bible with the additional context." FAILED. I even bought teaching Bibles, study Bibles that would break down scriptures and still failed to read cover to cover. With much prayer and the Holy Spirit's guidance, I decided to make reading the Bible, God's Word, a new year resolution. Surely, when I decided to say YES to Christ and be totally ALL IN, I clearly didn't know what to expect. I heard of how it was life-changing for others. But my reasons weren't for it to be life-changing, I wanted to be able to speak with authority, speak boldly and stand on God's Word for myself and upon sharing the gospel. How can I share the gospel, if I hadn't read the gospel? How can I speak with authority if I hadn't read the word of the Author? Upon saying yes, I was absolutely scared. Scared of the unknown, possible displacement from comfort zones within and outside of self, and not knowing what I'd be up against as Satan is always on his job trying to deter you from having a relationship with God.

Fear wasn't going to stop me because at the same time, I felt extremely excited knowing God, Jesus, and the Holy Spirit were involved. I knew I was to eventually face myself, come to terms with myself, get rid of some old ways that made me comfortable yet stuck. Oh, but I second guessed myself several times of being able to accomplish such a task. In my mind, the Bible represented the massiveness (if that's a word) of an elephant, with its thousands of pages, thousands of words, lil words, big words, riddles, not to mention the thought of trying to memorize scripture, who's who, who said what, who did what, etc. I literally had to convince myself over and over again that I could achieve. Once I said YES, I have thus made the commitment. I told myself, "ok, let's test this theory of reading the Bible can make me better", "be a witness for myself". Some may say that my mental process was silly or what's the big deal, you're only reading the Bible, but for me (and possibly others) this wasn't an easy feat and the big deal is spiritual transformation.

But hey, don't take my word for it, test God's Word for yourself.

In the following pages, I share insights from my personal journey of transformation through reading God's Word. Each topic is presented in a study guide format, offering practical self-help for Christians seeking to establish, define, or deepen their relationship with God.

The biblical scriptures referenced are from the New International Version (NIV), a popular and widely used translation for teaching and study.

ACKNOWLEDGEMENT

First and foremost, I give all glory and honor to God the Father whose guidance, wisdom, and grace has made this work possible. Thank you for the strength to persevere, the inspiration to create, and the countless blessings that have carried me through this journey. This work is a reflection of Your love and faithfulness, and I am forever grateful. I love you!

To my husband, Adam, thank you for always being there for me. Your unconditional love, encouragement, patience, and support has made/makes a significant difference in my life. I love you and am forever grateful. To my four beautiful children, Janaevia, Jamohri, Jachin, and Javari thank you for your undying love, support, and allowing me to be Mommy in every aspect of your lives. I love and am extremely proud of each of you.

To my family and friends, thank you for your unwavering support and encouragement throughout this journey. To those who directly offered words of wisdom, a listening ear, a hug, or a helping hand, your kindness has been invaluable. To those who supported me indirectly (through prayers, understanding, or simply by believing in me) know that your impact was felt deeply. I am truly blessed to have each of you in my life, and this work is a testament to the love and inspiration you've given me.

To myself, I extend heartfelt gratitude for the perseverance, passion, and countless hours poured into this project. Thank you for embracing challenges, nurturing creativity, and staying committed even in moments of doubt. This work stands as a testament to your growth and determination. I love you!

Contents

J-01: Spiritual Warfare: Standing Strong in God's Victory p7
J-02: Death is Life: Embracing the Power of Surrender p13
J-03: Women Remain Silent In The Church: A Call for Context & Biblical Truth p18
J-04: The Power of Our Words: Understanding Swearing in Light of God's Word p23
J-05: Tethered by Relationship: Grieving for the Earthly & Eternal p29
J-06: Deep, Unconditional Love: Reflecting God's Heart p35
J-07: Be Aware of the Spiritual Enemy: Recognizing Satan's Tactics p41
J-08: Shared Perspective: Impure Spirits (Luke 4:31-35) p47
J-09: Shared Perspective: Remarkable Things (Luke 5:26) p49
J-10: Shared Perspective: The Excitement of Jesus' Arrival & the Mystery of His Miracles p51
J-11: Shedding Parts of Self (John 15:1-2) p53
J-12: Holy Spirit, The Advocate (John 16:12-15) p58
J-13: Patience and Faith: Trusting God's Timing p64
J-14: Peace of Mind: Anchored in God's Presence p70
J-15: Overcoming Life's Tests: Embracing God's Strength p76
J-16: Independent and Leaning into Friendship Circles p82
J-17: Letting Go of Strongholds: Finding Freedom in Christ p88
J-18: Self-Love 🩶: Embracing Your God-Given Worth p94
J-19: Understanding What a Blessing Is from God p100
J-20: The Trinity: God the Father, the Son & the Holy Spirit p106
J-21: What to Do When God Tells You to Move p112
J-22: Heaven Revealed p118
J-23: Renew Mindset or Self-Sabotage p124
J-24: What to Do When You Can't Distinguish God's Voice p129
J-25: Experiencing a Loss: Finding God in Grief p135
J-26: In Silence Comes Wisdom p140

J=Journey

Contents cont.

J-27: Nourishing Your Needs p146
J-28: Discovering Your Path p152
J-29: Spiritual Evolution: Growing in Faith & Maturity p158
J-30: Growing Into Your Wonderful Self p164
J-31: How Not to Become an Exhausting Person Unto God p170
J-32: Human Being vs. Human Doing p176
J-33: Celebrate Self: Embracing Your God-Given Identity p182
J-34: Eliminating Habits & Vices of Sin p188
J-35: Jesus: The Way, The Truth, The Messenger p194
J-36: Journey of Reading God's Word: Walking in Truth & Growth .p199

J=Journey

J-1: Spiritual Warfare: Standing Strong in God's Victory

J-1: Prelude

In 2023, I reached a point where I was ready to let go of the strongholds that had affected me deeply—internally and subconsciously. If you've read my book, *Deprived Truth, Deprived Identity*, you'd understand. For years, I had learned to cope with pain, hurt, lack, abandonment, lies, and betrayal by compacting it all and tucking it away in an imaginary storage unit in my heart. I functioned as though none of it had any effect on me.

I believed I had undergone a long process of internal healing and "letting go." I had handed out forgiveness as though it was final, confident that I was free. But that "storage unit" in my heart told a different story. In my mind, I thought I had let go, but my heart hadn't fully released it all.

At the same time, I felt a growing, desperate desire for a deeper relationship with God. So, I took the first step: I recommitted my life to Christ. The next step was to commit to reading God's Word—cover to cover. Once I made those commitments, the spiritual warfare began.

On January 1, 2024, I had a profound, unexpected, and literal experience of spiritual deliverance. I had witnessed others undergo deliverance but had never experienced it myself. What I went through was beyond intense—an encounter that was powerful, freeing, and life-changing. From that day forward, I am truly free of those strongholds.

While I have been set free, the spiritual warfare has not ceased. What follows in this journey are the specific insights and revelations I have gained as God continues to transform me through His Word.

Title: Spiritual Warfare: Standing Strong in God's Victory

Introduction: The Battle You Cannot Ignore

As we approach a new day, a new month, a new year, let us recognize a profound truth: we are in the midst of a spiritual war. Ephesians 6:12 reminds us, "For we do not wrestle against flesh and blood, but against principalities, against powers, against the rulers of the darkness of this age, against spiritual hosts of wickedness in the heavenly places." The spiritual realm is active, and ignoring it leaves us vulnerable. However, God has equipped us with the weapons we need to stand firm and emerge victorious.

These notes will equip you to understand spiritual warfare, recognize the schemes of the enemy, and walk boldly in the victory already secured for you through Christ.

Main Points

I. Defining Spiritual Warfare

Spiritual warfare is the ongoing battle between God's kingdom and the forces of darkness. This is not a battle of physical might but one fought in the spiritual realm.

The Enemy: Satan and his demonic forces seek to deceive, destroy, and deviate us from God's purpose (1 Peter 5:8).

The Victory: Jesus Christ has already won the ultimate victory on the cross (Colossians 2:15). Our role is to stand firm in His triumph.

II. The Weapons of Our Warfare: Ephesians 6:10-18

Paul outlines the armor of God as our defense against spiritual attacks. Each piece is vital:

1. The Belt of Truth: Stand firm in God's Word, rejecting the lies of the enemy (John 8:32).

2. The Breastplate of Righteousness: Guard your heart and live in alignment with God's will (Proverbs 4:23).

3. The Shoes of Peace: Walk confidently in the peace that comes from the Gospel (John 14:27).

4. The Shield of Faith: Deflect the fiery darts of doubt, fear, and temptation (Hebrews 11:6).

5. The Helmet of Salvation: Protect your mind with the assurance of your salvation (Romans 12:2).

6. The Sword of the Spirit: Attack with the Word of God, your offensive weapon against lies and temptation (Hebrews 4:12).

7. Prayer: The lifeline connecting us to God's power and wisdom (Philippians 4:6-7).

III. The Tactics of the Enemy

The devil operates through deception, division, distraction, and discouragement.

1. Deception: Satan twists God's truth to sow doubt (Genesis 3:1).

2. Division: He seeks to divide relationships—families, churches, and communities (Matthew 12:25).

3. Distraction: The enemy uses worldly desires and busyness to pull us away from God (1 John 2:16).

4. Discouragement: He whispers lies that we are not good enough, loved, or forgiven (Revelation 12:10).

A Story of Victory: David and Goliath

In 1 Samuel 17, David faced a seemingly insurmountable enemy. Yet he declared, "The battle is the Lord's" (1 Samuel 17:47). David's victory over Goliath is a powerful reminder that spiritual battles are not won by human strength but by faith in God's power.

IV. The Revelation: Victory is Already Ours

Christ's death and resurrection secured the ultimate victory. Romans 8:37 declares, "In all these things we are more than conquerors through Him who loved us." When we stand in Christ, we fight from a place of victory, not defeat.

God is saying:

- "You are not alone." I will never leave you or forsake you (Deuteronomy 31:6).
- "You are empowered." My Spirit dwells in you, giving you strength to overcome (Romans 8:11).
- "You are victorious." No weapon formed against you shall prosper (Isaiah 54:17)

Application/Solutions: How to Fight and Win

1. Know Your Authority: Declare the authority you have in Christ: "I have given you authority... to overcome all the power of the enemy"
(Luke 10:19).
2. Stay Alert: Be sober and vigilant, watching for the enemy's schemes
(1 Peter 5:8).
3. Speak God's Word: Use Scripture to counter every lie, just as Jesus did during His temptation (Matthew 4:4).
4. Maintain a Life of Prayer: Pray without ceasing, seeking God's guidance and strength (1 Thessalonians 5:17).
5. Walk in Unity: Strengthen one another in the faith, standing together against the enemy (Ecclesiastes 4:12).
6. Resist the Devil: Submit to God and actively resist Satan's influence (James 4:7).

What God Wants You to Know

- "I am your defender." Stand still and watch how I fight for you (Exodus 14:14).
- "I am your strength." Lean on Me when you feel weak and weary (Isaiah 40:29).
- "I am your victory." Through Me, you can do all things (Philippians 4:13).

Conclusion
Walking Victoriously

This day, this month, this year, choose to stand firm in the victory of Jesus Christ. Suit up in the full armor of God, resist the schemes of the enemy, and walk boldly into the future God has prepared for you. As you face spiritual battles, remember: you are not fighting for victory—you are fighting from victory. Declare boldly, "If God is for me, who can be against me?" (Romans 8:31).

Your triumph is already secured. Step into each day with confidence, knowing that no weapon formed against you will prosper. Victory is yours!

J-2: Death is Life: Embracing the Power of Surrender

J-2: Prelude

Death to self, service before self—just as Jesus Christ demonstrated for me, you, and all of us. It's no longer about me; it's about sharing the Gospel. Jesus made it about each of us, and now, individually and collectively, we must make it about Him.

Title: Death is Life: Embracing the Power of Surrender

Introduction

• Main Idea: As believers, death is not the end but a doorway to true life. In both physical and spiritual contexts, dying to ourselves and the world allows us to experience the abundant life Christ offers.

• Scripture Reference: John 12:24 – "Very truly I tell you, unless a kernel of wheat falls to the ground and dies, it remains only a single seed. But if it dies, it produces many seeds."

• Purpose: To help believers understand the transformative nature of spiritual death and its power to bring eternal life and freedom in Christ.

Main Points

I. The Concept of Death in Scripture

• Physical Death as Transition: For believers, physical death is a passage to eternal life with God.
  • 2 Corinthians 5:8 – "To be absent from the body is to be present with the Lord."

• Spiritual Death to Sin: Dying to sin allows us to live in righteousness.
  • Romans 6:6-7 – "For we know that our old self was crucified with Him so that the body ruled by sin might be done away with, that we should no longer be slaves to sin."

II. Dying to Self Brings True Life

• Surrendering to God: When we lay down our desires and take up our cross daily, we find purpose and fulfillment.
  • Matthew 16:24-25 – "Whoever wants to be my disciple must deny themselves and take up their cross and follow me. For whoever wants to save their life will lose it, but whoever loses their life for me will find it."

- Living by the Spirit: Death to the flesh opens the door to life in the Spirit.
  - Galatians 2:20 – "I have been crucified with Christ and I no longer live, but Christ lives in me."

III. Death as the Path to Resurrection Power

- Jesus as the Ultimate Example: His death brought life to all who believe.
  - John 11:25-26 – "I am the resurrection and the life. The one who believes in me will live, even though they die."

- Personal Resurrection: Suffering, sacrifice, and dying to self lead to a new, abundant life in Christ.
  - 2 Timothy 2:11-12 – "If we died with Him, we will also live with Him."

Application/Solutions
How to Embrace the Life Found in Death:

1. Die to Sin Daily: Repent and surrender areas of sin to God.
   - Romans 8:13 – "If by the Spirit you put to death the misdeeds of the body, you will live."

2. Carry Your Cross: Commit to living sacrificially for Christ.
   - Luke 14:27 – "Whoever does not carry their cross and follow me cannot be my disciple."

3. Live by the Spirit: Seek God's guidance and power through prayer and Scripture.
   - Galatians 5:25 – "Since we live by the Spirit, let us keep in step with the Spirit."

4. Look to Eternity: Keep your focus on the eternal rewards of following Christ.
   - Colossians 3:2 – "Set your minds on things above, not on earthly things."

Conclusion

- Summary: Physical death ushers believers into eternal life with God, while spiritual death to sin and self ushers us into abundant life in Christ. Through surrender, we experience resurrection power and a life of freedom, purpose, and eternal joy.

- Encouragement: Remember, in God's kingdom, death is not the end but the beginning. Jesus promises: "I have come that they may have life, and have it to the full" (John 10:10).

- Call to Action: Embrace each day ready to die to yourself and the world so that you can fully embrace the life God has prepared for you.

These notes encourage believers to see death not as a loss but as a vital step toward experiencing the fullness of life in Christ.

J-3: Women Remain Silent In The Church: A Call for Context & Biblical Truth

J-3: Prelude

"What do you mean women are supposed to be quiet—like hush quiet?" Oh, I had a problem with this. I don't like being silenced by anyone. As children, our voices were often silenced or limited. We grew up lacking the confidence to express ourselves or the knowledge of how to do so.

Let me give you an example: in my generation, children knew their place. If they didn't, they were quickly reminded of it. "Stay out of grown folks' business," they'd say. Butting in on adult conversations could feel like a life-or-death situation. "Speak when spoken to" was the rule, but even then, you proceeded cautiously for fear of being backhanded.

So, as an adult, ain't no "shushing me" over here! That mindset didn't shift until I studied what God's Word says about women being silent in the church.

Title: Women Remain Silent In The Church: A Call for Context & Biblical Truth

Introduction

- Main Idea: The phrase "women should remain silent in the church" (1 Corinthians 14:34-35) has been widely debated. To understand its meaning, we must examine the cultural and historical context, the broader message of Scripture, and how it aligns with God's design for men and women in the church.

- Scripture Reference: 1 Corinthians 14:34-35 – "Women should remain silent in the churches. They are not allowed to speak but must be in submission, as the law says."

- Purpose: To clarify the meaning of this passage, reconcile it with the Bible's teachings on women's roles, and provide guidance for living in obedience to God's Word.

Main Points

I. The Cultural and Historical Context of Corinth

Background of the Corinthian Church:

- Corinth was a diverse and chaotic city with various religious and cultural influences. Disorder in worship was common in the early church, leading Paul to address this issue in 1 Corinthians 14.
- Paul's emphasis in the chapter was on orderly worship (1 Corinthians 14:33 – "For God is not a God of disorder but of peace.").

Role of Women in Corinth:

- In Corinthian society, women were often uneducated and culturally expected to take a submissive role in public forums. Paul's instruction may have been a corrective to maintain order, not a universal prohibition.

II. Biblical Examples of Women in Ministry
Women as Leaders and Prophets:
- Deborah – A judge and prophet who led Israel (Judges 4:4-5).
- Priscilla – A teacher of Apollos, alongside her husband Aquila (Acts 18:26).
- Phoebe – A deacon commended by Paul (Romans 16:1-2).
- Joel 2:28 – "Your sons and daughters will prophesy," showing God's inclusion of women in proclaiming His Word.

Women in the Early Church:
- Women played significant roles in supporting and spreading the gospel, such as Mary Magdalene, who was the first to witness and proclaim Jesus' resurrection (John 20:18).

III. Reconciling the Passage with Paul's Teachings
Focus on Order, Not Exclusion:
- 1 Corinthians 14:34-35 must be understood in light of 1 Corinthians 11:5, where Paul acknowledges women praying and prophesying in the church, provided they do so with respect for established norms.
- Paul's instruction was not to silence all women permanently but to address specific disruptions in the Corinthian church.

Equality in Christ:
- Galatians 3:28 – "There is neither Jew nor Gentile, neither slave nor free, nor is there male and female, for you are all one in Christ Jesus."

IV. Application for the Modern Church
Principles of Order and Respect:
- The core message is about maintaining order in worship and respect for authority, applicable to both men and women.

Encouraging Women in Ministry:
- The church should affirm and empower women to use their God-given gifts for His glory.
- Women should study Scripture and seek opportunities to serve in teaching, leadership, and other roles, in alignment with biblical principles.

Application/Solutions

1. Study Scripture in Context:
- Approach challenging passages with prayer and a willingness to explore cultural and historical context (2 Timothy 2:15).

2. Encourage Women's Ministry:
- Acknowledge and support the contributions of women in teaching, leading, and serving in the church.

3. Promote Order in Worship:
- Ensure all church practices reflect the principles of unity, respect, and glorification of God (Colossians 3:16-17).

Conclusion

- **Summary:** The instruction for women to "remain silent" in 1 Corinthians 14 was not a universal prohibition but a call to maintain order in worship. Scripture affirms the valuable roles of women in ministry and their equality in Christ.

- **Encouragement:** Women are called to use their gifts boldly for God's glory while honoring the principles of Scripture.

- **Call to Action:** Embrace each day with a renewed understanding of God's purpose for both men and women, working together to build His kingdom in unity and love.

These notes clarify the text, honors biblical principles, and empowers both men and women to serve effectively in the body of Christ.

J-4: The Power of Our Words: Understanding Swearing in Light of God's Word

J-4: Prelude

Swearing and cursing were normal parts of my life growing up. Swearing was often used as a way to prove you were telling the truth. For example, if a story sounded far-fetched, we'd say things like, "I swear on my momma," "on my grandmother," or anyone of significance to us.

Swearing wasn't as frequent back then because we were taught it wasn't necessarily a good thing, but it wasn't seen as terrible either. At least, that's what I thought. While writing about swearing, I discovered Hebrews 6:13-16 during my daily Bible reading:

> "When God made His promise to Abraham, since there was no one greater for Him to swear by, He swore by Himself..."

This passage showed me that even God swore—on Himself. It solidified the understanding that swearing, as described in this context, confirms an oath. However, this raised a question in my heart: is swearing unfavorable in God's eyes?

Curse words, though, are another matter. Cursing became a form of communication—sometimes used to emphasize seriousness or vent anger. It was what I heard daily growing up. I didn't use the harshest ones but excused my occasional use by saying, "If it's in the Bible, surely I can say it." Truthfully, not everything needs repeating.

Reading God's Word taught me about the power of the tongue. Transformation accepted.

Title: The Power of Our Words: Understanding Swearing in Light of God's Word

Introduction

- Main Idea: Our words have the power to build up or tear down, to glorify God or dishonor Him. Swearing, whether in cursing or using God's name in vain, reflects the condition of our hearts and the respect we have for Him.

- Scripture Reference: Matthew 12:36-37 – "But I tell you that everyone will have to give account on the day of judgment for every empty word they have spoken. For by your words you will be acquitted, and by your words you will be condemned."

- Purpose: To explore what the Bible says about swearing, understand its spiritual implications, and learn how to align our speech with God's will.

Main Points

I. What Does the Bible Say About Swearing?

Using God's Name in Vain:

- Exodus 20:7 – "You shall not misuse the name of the Lord your God, for the Lord will not hold anyone guiltless who misuses His name."
- Misusing God's name in oaths, casual speech, or anger shows irreverence toward His holiness.

Profanity and Corrupt Speech:

- Ephesians 4:29 – "Do not let any unwholesome talk come out of your mouths, but only what is helpful for building others up."
- Swearing and vulgar language are unwholesome and unfit for those representing Christ.

Truthful Speech Over Oaths:
- Matthew 5:34-37 – Jesus taught, "Do not swear an oath at all… All you need to say is simply 'Yes' or 'No'; anything beyond this comes from the evil one."
- James 5:12 - Above all, my brothers and sisters, do not swear—not by heaven or by earth or by anything else. All you need to say is a simple "Yes" or "No." Otherwise you will be condemned.

II. The Spiritual Implications of Swearing

Reflects the Heart's Condition:
- Luke 6:45 – "The mouth speaks what the heart is full of." Swearing reveals anger, bitterness, or irreverence residing in the heart.

Affects Our Witness:
- Colossians 4:6 – "Let your conversation be always full of grace, seasoned with salt, so that you may know how to answer everyone."
- Our speech impacts how others perceive Christ through us. Swearing can hinder our testimony.

III. Transforming Our Speech to Honor God

Speaking Words of Life:
- Proverbs 18:21 – "The tongue has the power of life and death." Use words to encourage, edify, and bless others.

Replacing Swearing with Praise and Gratitude:
- Psalm 34:1 – "I will bless the Lord at all times; His praise shall continually be in my mouth."
- Cultivate a habit of speaking praise and thanksgiving instead of profanity.

Guarding Our Hearts and Minds:
- Philippians 4:8 – "Whatever is true, noble, right, pure, lovely, admirable—if anything is excellent or praiseworthy—think about such things."

Application/Solutions
How to Overcome Swearing:

1. Recognize the Issue:
• Acknowledge that swearing dishonors God and seek His forgiveness.
 • 1 John 1:9 – "If we confess our sins, He is faithful and just to forgive us our sins and purify us from all unrighteousness."

2. Fill Your Heart with God's Word:
• Meditate on Scripture daily to renew your mind and speech.
 • Psalm 119:11 – "I have hidden Your word in my heart that I might not sin against You."

3. Choose Accountability:
• Surround yourself with believers who will encourage and correct you when needed.
 • Proverbs 27:17 – "As iron sharpens iron, so one person sharpens another."

4. Pray for Transformation:
• Ask God for help in controlling your tongue and changing your speech patterns.
 • James 3:8-10 – "No human being can tame the tongue. It is a restless evil, full of deadly poison."

Conclusion
• Summary: Swearing, whether through profanity or misusing God's name, dishonors Him and reveals the condition of our hearts. God calls us to use our words to glorify Him and build others up.

• Encouragement: With God's help, we can transform our speech to reflect His grace and love.

• Call to Action: Embrace each day with a commitment to honor God through your words. Declare, like David, "May the words of my mouth and the meditation of my heart be pleasing in Your sight, Lord, my Rock and my Redeemer" (Psalm 19:14).

These notes challenge believers to guard their words and use their speech as a reflection of God's holiness and love.

J-5: Tethered by Relationship: Grieving for the Earthly & Eternal

J-5: Prelude

At my stepdad's funeral—the only father I knew—I noticed family and friends expressing their emotions through tears and stories. As I observed, I became aware of another funeral happening in the next room. While I empathized with the grieving family, I felt unbothered by their loss.

That moment reminded me of the importance of relationships. Relationships are what we lean on, what we value, and what shape our lives. It also solidified something for me: the saying "blood is thicker than water" doesn't always hold true. It's the relationship that matters.

Title: Tethered by Relationship: Grieving for the Earthly & Eternal

Introduction

- Main Idea: Relationships are powerful and life-defining. When we lose someone we are tethered to, we grieve deeply because of the bond we shared. Similarly, our relationship with God through Jesus Christ should be so profound that when it weakens, we instinctively respond with deep spiritual grief.

- Scripture Reference: Matthew 22:37-39 – "Love the Lord your God with all your heart and with all your soul and with all your mind. This is the first and greatest commandment. And the second is like it: 'Love your neighbor as yourself.'"

- Purpose: To explore the importance of being tethered to God and others through relationships and to challenge believers to evaluate their connection with God.

Main Points

I. The Power of Relationships on Earth

Earthly Connections Are Deeply Personal:

- Relationships tether us emotionally, mentally, and spiritually to others.
- Example: At a funeral, we instinctively grieve for the loved one we knew, but not for a stranger in another room.
  - Romans 12:15 – "Rejoice with those who rejoice; mourn with those who mourn." Sympathy is natural, but true grief comes from personal connection.

Grief Is Individual but Equally Valid:

- Everyone grieves differently, but each form of grief is valid and intense.
  - Ecclesiastes 3:4 – "A time to weep and a time to laugh, a time to mourn and a time to dance."
- Our responses—whether crying, reminiscing, or withdrawing—are shaped by the depth of our relationships.

II. Grieving in the Absence of God

The Parallels Between Earthly and Spiritual Grief:

- When a loved one dies, we grieve their absence. Similarly, when our relationship with God weakens, we should feel an intense spiritual grief.
- Psalm 42:1-2 – "As the deer pants for streams of water, so my soul pants for you, my God. My soul thirsts for God, for the living God."

Signs of a Strained Relationship with God:

- Lack of prayer, diminished worship, loss of joy, and feelings of spiritual emptiness.
- Spiritual grief should prompt us to cry, pray, and take steps to restore our connection with Him.

III. Cultivating a Deep Relationship with God

Tether Yourself to God Through Christ:

- John 15:5 – "I am the vine; you are the branches. If you remain in me and I in you, you will bear much fruit; apart from me you can do nothing."
- A strong relationship with God requires daily communication, trust, and obedience.

Grieve When the Relationship Slips:

- Feel the weight of separation and take action to reconcile with God.
  - 2 Corinthians 7:10 – "Godly sorrow brings repentance that leads to salvation and leaves no regret, but worldly sorrow brings death."

Evaluate your relationship with God, is it strong, weak, or none at all. There is time, and the time is today, the time is now. "Yesterday" aka the past is gone, poof, vanished in thin air, can't get back, some of us can't even remember and that's ok, "tomorrow" aka the future doesn't even exist, how do you know there is going to be a tomorrow FOR YOU. So what we have and all that we have is today, right now at this moment. And to be honest, there is always room for improvement, SO IMPROVE.

Practical Steps to Strengthen Your Connection:
1. Pray Without Ceasing (1 Thessalonians 5:17).
2. Meditate on His Word (Psalm 119:11).
3. Worship in Spirit and Truth (John 4:24).
4. Confess and Repent of Sin (1 John 1:9).

Application/Solutions
Living Tethered to God and Others:
1. Value Your Earthly Relationships:
- Be present and intentional with loved ones.
- Reflect Christ's love in your interactions (John 13:34-35).

2. Pursue God Relentlessly:
- Treat your relationship with God as the most important bond in your life.
- Grieve deeply and take corrective action when you feel distant from Him.

3. Encourage Others to Reconnect with God:
- Share the importance of being tethered to God through Jesus Christ.
  - Hebrews 10:24-25 – "And let us consider how we may spur one another on toward love and good deeds, not giving up meeting together, as some are in the habit of doing, but encouraging one another."

Conclusion
- **Summary:** Just as earthly relationships tether us emotionally, our relationship with God should be the most important connection we have. When we drift away from Him, we should respond with spiritual grief and take steps to restore the bond.

- **Encouragement:** As you embark each day, prioritize your relationship with God. Stay tethered to Him through prayer, worship, and obedience.

- Call to Action: Reflect on your connection with God. If it feels distant, grieve the separation and commit to restoring it. Declare, like David, "Restore to me the joy of your salvation and grant me a willing spirit, to sustain me" (Psalm 51:12).

These notes remind us of the depth of human and divine relationships, urging us to stay connected to God with the same intensity we feel for our loved ones.

J-6: Deep, Unconditional Love: Reflecting God's Heart

J-6: Prelude

Do I place conditions on my love—for myself or others?

Title: Deep, Unconditional Love: Reflecting God's Heart

Introduction

- Main Idea: Deep, unconditional love reflects God's character and is the foundation of our faith. As we seize each day, it's vital to embrace and demonstrate this kind of love, both to God and to others.

- Scripture Reference: 1 John 4:7-8 – "Dear friends, let us love one another, for love comes from God. Everyone who loves has been born of God and knows God. Whoever does not love does not know God, because God is love."

- Purpose: To understand the depth of God's unconditional love, how it shapes our lives, and how we can share it with others.

Main Points

I. Understanding God's Deep, Unconditional Love

Definition of Unconditional Love:

- Love without conditions, requirements, or limitations. It is sacrificial and steadfast.
  - Romans 5:8 – "But God demonstrates His own love for us in this: While we were still sinners, Christ died for us."

God's Love in Action:

- The sending of His Son: John 3:16 – "For God so loved the world that He gave His one and only Son, that whoever believes in Him shall not perish but have eternal life."
- God's faithfulness: Lamentations 3:22-23 – "Because of the Lord's great love we are not consumed, for His compassions never fail. They are new every morning; great is your faithfulness."

II. Receiving and Embracing God's Love

Recognizing Our Worth in God's Eyes:

• Psalm 139:13-14 – "For you created my inmost being; you knit me together in my mother's womb. I praise you because I am fearfully and wonderfully made."

• Understanding God's love helps us overcome feelings of unworthiness and insecurity.

Responding to His Love:

• Through obedience: John 14:15 – "If you love me, keep my commands."

• By trusting Him: 1 Peter 5:7 – "Cast all your anxiety on Him because He cares for you."

III. Demonstrating Deep, Unconditional Love to Others

The Call to Love Others:

• John 13:34-35 – "A new command I give you: Love one another. As I have loved you, so you must love one another. By this everyone will know that you are my disciples, if you love one another."

• Loving others is a testimony of our relationship with Christ.

Practical Ways to Love Unconditionally:

1. Forgive Freely:
• Colossians 3:13 – "Bear with each other and forgive one another if any of you has a grievance against someone. Forgive as the Lord forgave you."

2. Serve Sacrificially:
• Galatians 5:13 – "Serve one another humbly in love."

3. Show Compassion:
• Ephesians 4:32 – "Be kind and compassionate to one another, forgiving each other, just as in Christ God forgave you."

4. Love Even Your Enemies:
• Matthew 5:44 – "But I tell you, love your enemies and pray for those who persecute you."

Application/Solutions
Living Out Deep, Unconditional Love Each Day:

1. Start with God:
- Spend time in prayer, worship, and meditating on His Word to deepen your understanding of His love.
  - Romans 8:38-39 – "For I am convinced that neither death nor life... will be able to separate us from the love of God that is in Christ Jesus our Lord."

2. Evaluate Your Relationships:
- Identify areas where you need to extend love, forgiveness, or compassion.
  - 1 Corinthians 13:4-7 – "Love is patient, love is kind... It always protects, always trusts, always hopes, always perseveres."

3. Practice Daily Acts of Love:
- Intentionally show love to family, friends, coworkers, and even strangers.
  - Hebrews 13:16 – "And do not forget to do good and to share with others, for with such sacrifices God is pleased."

4. Love in Challenging Situations:
- Commit to loving even when it's difficult or inconvenient.
  - Proverbs 10:12 – "Hatred stirs up conflict, but love covers over all wrongs."

Conclusion

- Summary: God's deep, unconditional love is the foundation of our faith and the model for how we are to love others. Each day, let us commit to receiving His love fully and sharing it freely.

- Encouragement: No matter where you are in life, God's love is constant, unchanging, and available to you. "The Lord your God is with you, the Mighty Warrior who saves. He will take great delight in you; in His love He will no longer rebuke you but will rejoice over you with singing" (Zephaniah 3:17).

• Call to Action: Begin each day by deepening your relationship with God and reflecting His unconditional love to everyone around you. Declare, "Let all that you do be done in love" (1 Corinthians 16:14).

These notes encourage believers to anchor their lives in God's love and live out that love toward others, making it a central theme as we embrace each day.

J-7: Be Aware of the Spiritual Enemy: Recognizing Satan's Tactics

J-7: Prelude

We often place ourselves in unwanted situations by moving without God's guidance. We take matters into our own hands instead of waiting on Him. But can we recognize when Satan is interfering?

Title: Be Aware of the Spiritual Enemy: Recognizing Satan's Tactics

Introduction

• Main Idea: As we embrace each day, it's crucial to recognize and understand the reality of our spiritual enemy, Satan. Awareness equips us to resist his schemes and walk victoriously in Christ.

• Scripture Reference: 1 Peter 5:8 – "Be alert and of sober mind. Your enemy the devil prowls around like a roaring lion looking for someone to devour."

• Purpose: To explore Satan's strategies, understand his limitations, and learn how to stand firm against his attacks with the power of God.

Main Points

I. Recognizing Satan's Identity and Mission

Who is Satan?

• Ezekiel 28:14-17: Satan was a created being, a fallen angel who rebelled against God due to pride.
• Isaiah 14:12-15: Known as Lucifer, he desired to exalt himself above God.

Satan's Mission:

• To steal, kill, and destroy: John 10:10.
• To deceive the world: Revelation 12:9 – "The great dragon was hurled down—that ancient serpent called the devil, or Satan, who leads the whole world astray."

II. Understanding Satan's Strategies

Deception:

• He distorts God's Word: Genesis 3:1 – "Did God really say...?"
• He masquerades as an angel of light: 2 Corinthians 11:14.

Temptation:
• He tempts us to sin by appealing to our desires: Matthew 4:1-11 – Jesus was tempted by Satan in the wilderness.

Accusation:
• He condemns and accuses believers: Revelation 12:10 – "...the accuser of our brothers and sisters."

Division:
• He sows discord among God's people: Proverbs 6:16-19.

III. Satan's Limitations
He is not omnipotent, omnipresent, or omniscient:
• Only God is all-powerful, all-knowing, and everywhere at once (Psalm 139:1-12).

He operates under God's authority:
• Job 1:12: Satan could only act within the boundaries set by God.

He is already defeated:
• Colossians 2:15 – "And having disarmed the powers and authorities, He made a public spectacle of them, triumphing over them by the cross."

IV. Standing Firm Against Satan's Attacks
Be Spiritually Alert:
• 1 Peter 5:8-9 – "Resist him, standing firm in the faith."
• Stay vigilant in prayer and discernment.

Use the Armor of God:
• Ephesians 6:10-18: Truth, righteousness, the gospel of peace, faith, salvation, the Word of God, and prayer.

Rely on God's Power:
• James 4:7 – "Submit yourselves, then, to God. Resist the devil, and he will flee from you."

Claim Victory Through Christ:
• Romans 16:20 – "The God of peace will soon crush Satan under your feet."

Application/Solutions
Practical Steps for each day:

1. Daily Spiritual Discipline:
• Pray regularly and read Scripture to fortify your mind and spirit.
   • Psalm 119:11 – "I have hidden your word in my heart that I might not sin against you."

2. Guard Your Thoughts:
• Take every thought captive: 2 Corinthians 10:5.
• Reject lies and replace them with God's truth.

3. Beware of those desiring to intimidate: Nehemiah 6:13 - He had been hired to intimidate me so that I would commit a sin by doing this, and then they would give me a bad name to discredit me.
• Remember, the enemy is always at work assigning those to manipulate and intimidate so that you/I may go against God's Word thus sinning and giving others an opportunity to discredit. Be mindful and keenly aware of your actions and the action of others; recognize the opps and position yourself to be led by God.

3. Cultivate a Community of Believers:
• Fellowship with others for encouragement and accountability: Hebrews 10:24-25.

4. Proclaim Christ's Victory:
• Speak God's promises over your life, declaring Satan's defeat.
  • Revelation 12:11 – "They triumphed over him by the blood of the Lamb and by the word of their testimony."

Conclusion

• Summary: Satan is a real enemy, but his power is limited, and his defeat is certain. By recognizing his tactics, equipping ourselves with God's armor, and staying rooted in Christ, we can resist his schemes and live victoriously.

• Encouragement: "The One who is in you is greater than the one who is in the world" (1 John 4:4).

• Call to Action: As you embrace each day, resolve to be spiritually vigilant and to walk boldly in the victory already won through Jesus Christ. Declare, "No weapon formed against me shall prosper" (Isaiah 54:17).

These notes encourage believers to remain spiritually aware, equip themselves for spiritual warfare, and rely on Christ's power to overcome the enemy each day.

J-8: Shared Perspective: Impure Spirits (Luke 4:31-35)

Title: Shared Perspective: Impure Spirits

Luke 4:31-35 – Jesus Drives Out an Impure Spirit

"31 Then he went down to Capernaum, a town in Galilee, and on the Sabbath he taught the people.
32 They were amazed at his teaching, because his words had authority.
33 In the synagogue, there was a man possessed by a demon, an impure spirit. He cried out at the top of his voice,
34 "Go away! What do you want with us, Jesus of Nazareth? Have you come to destroy us? I know who you are—the Holy One of God!"
35 "Be quiet!" Jesus said sternly. "Come out of him!" Then the demon threw the man down before them all and came out without injuring him."

My Reflection:

Even in the house of God, we sometimes encounter individuals who are wearing masks—pretenders among us. But just as Jesus demonstrated in this passage, we are called to recognize and confront the unclean spirits that attempt to operate within us or among us.

The Bible teaches us to call upon the name of Jesus, rebuke those spirits, and trust in His authority. As Scripture assures us, when we speak with faith in Jesus' name, the unclean spirits have no choice but to flee.

Let us walk in boldness and authority, trusting that the same power Jesus displayed is available to us through His Holy Spirit.

J-9: Shared Perspective: Remarkable Things (Luke 5:26)

Title: Shared Perspective: Remarkable Things

Luke 5:26 – "We have seen remarkable things today."

My Reflection:
Each day we wake up, we witness remarkable things.

A remarkable thing: I woke up today.

But it doesn't stop there. Remarkable things abound:

I woke up today with new breath.

I woke up today with new life.

I woke up today with new grace.

I woke up today with new mercy.

I woke up today with a new start.

And most importantly, I woke up today with God, with Jesus, and with the Holy Spirit.

Surely, all these things are not just remarkable—they are extraordinary expressions of God's love and faithfulness.

J-10: Shared Perspective: The Excitement of Jesus' Arrival & the Mystery of His Miracles

Title: Shared Perspective: The Excitement of Jesus' Arrival & the Mystery of His Miracles

As I began reading through the Gospels—Matthew, Mark, Luke, and John—I felt an overwhelming sense of excitement. I thought to myself, "Jesus is here!"

But as I read on, something stood out to me: every time Jesus healed someone, He often instructed them, "Don't tell anyone." This made me pause and ask, "Why would Jesus say that?"

Every day, God is performing miracles right before our eyes. Think about it—when He answers a specific prayer, pours out an unexpected blessing, or carries us through trials and tribulations, giving us victory, we naturally want to share it. I know I do! I can't help but tell somebody, then another person, and yet another, about His goodness and what He's done for me.

So, why did Jesus ask those He healed to keep quiet? This question lingered in my heart. I began to reflect and dig deeper (as Scripture says, "Seek and you will find"). Finally, I came to understand His reasoning.

Jesus wasn't dismissing the miracles or the joy they brought. Instead, He sought to avoid unnecessary attention that could hinder His mission. He wanted to ensure His focus remained on teaching, preaching, and sharing the true message of His ministry: spiritual salvation. The miracles were not the central focus but a sign pointing to God's greater plan of redemption.

Now I see it so clearly. Jesus wanted people to understand that His mission wasn't just about healing the body—it was about transforming the soul. What a profound lesson for us all!

J-11: Shedding Parts of Self (John 15:1-2)

J-11: Prelude

For years, I wrestled with feelings of inadequacy, failure, and worthlessness—born from rejection and wrapped in insecurity. These struggles distorted my sense of identity, shaped by harsh judgments and subtle acceptance of the enemy's lies.

In February 2024, I joined a five-week mentorship workshop, *Looking in the Mirror*, led by an inspiring Spiritual Life Coach. Through reflection, study, and the practical application of God's Word, I rediscovered my identity in Christ. I confronted the thoughts, words, and behaviors that contributed to my fractured self-image.

The result? I embraced the truth of who God says I am and experienced life-changing freedom.

Title: Shedding Parts of Self (John 15:1-2)

Introduction

- Main Idea: As we embrace each day, God calls us to a deeper level of growth and fruitfulness by pruning away parts of ourselves that hinder His work in our lives.

- Scripture Reference: John 15:1-2 – "I am the true vine, and my Father is the gardener. He cuts off every branch in me that bears no fruit, while every branch that does bear fruit He prunes so that it will be even more fruitful."

- Purpose: To understand the necessity of spiritual pruning, identify areas in our lives that need to be "shedded," and embrace God's process for greater fruitfulness in the new year.

Main Points

I. The Vine and the Gardener

Jesus as the True Vine:

- John 15:5 – "I am the vine; you are the branches." Our spiritual life depends on staying connected to Jesus.
- Just as a vine supplies nutrients to its branches, Jesus nourishes us spiritually.

God as the Gardener:

- He carefully tends to us, knowing what needs to be removed for optimal growth.
  - Isaiah 64:8 – "We are the clay, you are the potter; we are all the work of your hand."

II. The Purpose of Pruning

Pruning Removes What is Unfruitful:

- Hebrews 12:1 – "Let us throw off everything that hinders and the sin that so easily entangles."
- Dead branches (habits, relationships, or attitudes) drain our energy and prevent growth.

Pruning Enhances Fruitfulness:
• Galatians 5:22-23 – The fruit of the Spirit (love, joy, peace, patience, etc.) grows as we submit to God's pruning.
• Cutting away the unnecessary allows us to focus on God's purpose for our lives.

III. The Pain and Promise of Pruning

The Pain of Pruning:
• Pruning often feels like loss: letting go of comfort zones, sinful habits, or toxic relationships.
  • 2 Corinthians 12:9 – "My grace is sufficient for you, for my power is made perfect in weakness."

The Promise of Growth:
• Psalm 1:3 – "That person is like a tree planted by streams of water, which yields its fruit in season."
• Pruning is evidence of God's investment in us. He prunes what He intends to grow.

Application/Solutions

How to Embrace God's Pruning:

1. Identify What Needs to Be Shedded:
• Ask God to reveal areas of your life that are unfruitful.
  • Psalm 139:23-24 – "Search me, God, and know my heart; test me and know my anxious thoughts."

2. Submit to the Process:
• Trust God's wisdom even when the pruning feels painful.
  • Proverbs 3:5-6 – "Trust in the Lord with all your heart and lean not on your own understanding."

3. Stay Connected to the Vine:
• Daily prayer, Bible study, and obedience are vital to maintaining spiritual nourishment.
  • John 15:4 – "Remain in me, as I also remain in you."

4. Bear Witness to the Fruit:
• Share your testimony of transformation with others to encourage their faith.
  • Matthew 5:16 – "Let your light shine before others, that they may see your good deeds and glorify your Father in heaven."

Conclusion

• Summary: Pruning is a vital part of God's work in our lives. By shedding parts of ourselves that hinder growth, we allow God to produce abundant fruit through us.

• Encouragement: Trust that God's pruning is not punishment but preparation for greater fruitfulness.

• Call to Action: Declare, "Lord, prune what hinders me so I can be fruitful for Your glory."

Reflection Questions

1. What habits, relationships, or attitudes is God asking you to let go of?
2. How can you stay more deeply connected to Jesus, the true vine, this year?
3. What fruits of the Spirit do you desire to grow in your life in the new year?

These notes encourage believers to embrace God's pruning process for spiritual growth and fruitfulness, trusting His wisdom as they embrace each day.

J-12: Holy Spirit, The Advocate
(John 16:12-15)

J-12: Prelude

In January 2024, God told me to resign from my career of 22 years. My initial reaction was disbelief. "I'm earning a six-figure income, established in my field, and supporting my family," I thought. But this wasn't about money or materialism—it was about my independence.

I struggled with discerning God's voice versus the enemy's interference. Then God reminded me, "Didn't I provide for you when you left the military? Where is your faith?" Despite this, I remained disobedient for months.

By June 2024, God told me again to leave. This time, I obeyed. Was I scared? Yes. Was my independence stripped away? Yes. But God has provided for every need.

Title: Holy Spirit, The Advocate (John 16:12-15)

Introduction

- Main Idea: As you prepare for each day or the new year, it is essential to reflect on the role of the Holy Spirit as our Advocate, who leads us into truth, reveals Christ's will, and empowers us to live victoriously.

- Scripture Reference: John 16:12-15 – Jesus says, "I have much more to say to you, more than you can now bear. But when He, the Spirit of truth, comes, He will guide you into all the truth. He will not speak on His own; He will speak only what He hears, and He will tell you what is yet to come."

- Purpose: To understand the transformative power of the Holy Spirit in guiding, teaching, and revealing God's truth in our lives.

Main Points
I. The Role of the Holy Spirit

1. The Spirit of Truth:
- John 14:26 – "The Advocate, the Holy Spirit, whom the Father will send in My name, will teach you all things and remind you of everything I have said to you."
- The Holy Spirit communicates divine truth, bringing clarity to God's Word and revealing His will for us.

2. The Spirit as the Advocate:
- An advocate is one who supports, defends, and pleads on behalf of another.
  - Romans 8:26 – "The Spirit helps us in our weakness. We do not know what we ought to pray for, but the Spirit Himself intercedes for us through wordless groans."

II. The Work of the Holy Spirit in Believers

1. Guides Us Into All Truth:
- The Holy Spirit leads believers into spiritual understanding.
  - 1 Corinthians 2:10 – "These are the things God has revealed to us by His Spirit. The Spirit searches all things, even the deep things of God."
- He illuminates our minds to recognize God's purpose and discern His will.

2. Speaks Only What He Hears:
- The Spirit does not act independently but communicates what He hears from the Father and the Son.
  - John 5:19 – Jesus modeled this same submission, saying, "The Son can do nothing by Himself; He can do only what He sees His Father doing."

3. Reveals What is to Come:
- The Holy Spirit equips us to prepare for future challenges and blessings.
  - Amos 3:7 – "Surely the Sovereign Lord does nothing without revealing His plan to His servants the prophets."

III. Glorifies Christ Through Us

1. Magnifies Jesus:
- John 16:14 – "He will glorify Me because it is from Me that He will receive what He will make known to you."
- The Spirit's ultimate purpose is to point us to Christ and deepen our relationship with Him.

2. Empowers Us for Kingdom Work:
- Acts 1:8 – "But you will receive power when the Holy Spirit comes on you; and you will be My witnesses in Jerusalem, and in all Judea and Samaria, and to the ends of the earth."
- The Spirit gives us boldness to proclaim the Gospel and live out our faith.

Application/Solutions
How to Embrace the Holy Spirit's Role:

1. Acknowledge His Presence Daily:
• Pray for the Spirit's guidance and yield to His leading.
 • Psalm 143:10 – "Teach me to do Your will, for You are my God; may Your good Spirit lead me on level ground."

2. Listen to His Voice:
• Spend time in prayer and the Word to attune your heart to His promptings.
 • Isaiah 30:21 – "Whether you turn to the right or to the left, your ears will hear a voice behind you, saying, 'This is the way; walk in it.'"

3. Submit to His Refining Work:
• Allow the Spirit to shape your character and strip away anything that hinders your relationship with God.
 • Galatians 5:22-23 – Cultivate the fruit of the Spirit: love, joy, peace, patience, kindness, goodness, faithfulness, gentleness, and self-control.

4. Walk in Boldness:
• Trust the Spirit to empower you in your calling and strengthen you in challenges.
 • 2 Timothy 1:7 – "For the Spirit God gave us does not make us timid, but gives us power, love, and self-discipline."

Conclusion

• Summary: The Holy Spirit, our Advocate, plays a vital role in our spiritual growth by guiding us into truth, revealing God's will, and glorifying Christ through our lives.

• Encouragement: As you embrace each day, let us deepen our relationship with the Holy Spirit, trusting Him to lead us into a year of transformation and fruitfulness.

- Call to Action: Declare, "Holy Spirit, I invite You to lead, teach, and empower me as I embrace each day."

Reflection Questions

1. How can you become more aware of the Holy Spirit's presence in your daily life?
2. What areas of your life need the guidance and truth of the Spirit?
3. How can you allow the Holy Spirit to glorify Christ through your actions and words?

These notes highlight the Holy Spirit's indispensable role as our Advocate and challenges us to actively engage with Him for spiritual growth in our daily walk.

J-13: Patience and Faith: Trusting God's Timing

J-13: Prelude

When I resigned, I trusted God had something greater in store for me, but I had no idea what. I've applied for countless jobs only to face rejection. This process has taught me patience, trust, and the importance of aligning myself with God's Word and promises.

Title: Patience and Faith: Trusting God's Timing

Introduction

- Main Idea: As we approach each day, patience and faith are essential virtues to carry forward. Faith anchors us in God's promises, and patience sustains us as we wait for His perfect timing.

- Scripture Reference: Hebrews 10:36 – "You need to persevere so that when you have done the will of God, you will receive what He has promised."

- Purpose: To encourage believers to trust in God's timing, grow in patience, and strengthen their faith as they navigate life's challenges.

Main Points

I. Understanding Patience and Faith

1. Patience Defined:
- Waiting calmly and confidently for God's plan to unfold.
  - Psalm 37:7 – "Be still before the Lord and wait patiently for Him."

2. Faith Defined:
- Trusting in God's character and promises, even when we don't see immediate results.
  - Hebrews 11:1 – "Now faith is confidence in what we hope for and assurance about what we do not see."

II. Biblical Examples of Patience and Faith

1. Abraham:
- Genesis 12:1-4 – God promises Abraham descendants, but he must wait 25 years for Isaac's birth.
- Abraham's faith was credited to him as righteousness (Romans 4:20-22).

2. Job:
- Job endured immense suffering but remained faithful, trusting in God's sovereignty.
  - James 5:11 – "You have heard of Job's perseverance and have seen what the Lord finally brought about. The Lord is full of compassion and mercy."

3. Jesus:
- Jesus demonstrated patience in His ministry, awaiting the fulfillment of God's redemptive plan.
  - 1 Peter 2:23 – "When they hurled their insults at Him, He did not retaliate; when He suffered, He made no threats. Instead, He entrusted Himself to Him who judges justly."

III. The Role of Patience in Faith

1. Patience Refines Us:
- Trials and waiting develop spiritual maturity.
  - James 1:3-4 – "The testing of your faith produces perseverance. Let perseverance finish its work so that you may be mature and complete, not lacking anything."

2. Patience Strengthens Trust in God:
- Waiting deepens our reliance on God and His timing.
  - Isaiah 40:31 – "But those who hope in the Lord will renew their strength. They will soar on wings like eagles; they will run and not grow weary, they will walk and not be faint."

3. Patience Protects Us from Rash Decisions:
- Acting prematurely can lead to setbacks, but patience allows God's plan to unfold.
  - Proverbs 19:2 – "Desire without knowledge is not good—how much more will hasty feet miss the way!"

Application/Solutions
How to Cultivate Patience and Faith:

1. Meditate on God's Promises:
- Reflect on scriptures that remind you of God's faithfulness.
  - Psalm 27:14 – "Wait for the Lord; be strong and take heart and wait for the Lord."

2. Pray for Strength:
- Ask God to help you trust His timing and grow in patience.
  - Philippians 4:6-7 – "Do not be anxious about anything, but in every situation, by prayer and petition, with thanksgiving, present your requests to God."

3. Lean on the Holy Spirit:
- The Spirit produces patience as a fruit in your life.
  - Galatians 5:22-23 – "But the fruit of the Spirit is love, joy, peace, forbearance, kindness, goodness, faithfulness, gentleness, and self-control."

4. Stay Active in Faith:
- While waiting, remain obedient and committed to what God has called you to do.
  - Colossians 3:23 – "Whatever you do, work at it with all your heart, as working for the Lord, not for human masters."

5. Encourage Others:
- Share your testimony of waiting on God to strengthen others.
  - 1 Thessalonians 5:11 – "Therefore encourage one another and build each other up."

Conclusion

Summary: Patience and faith go hand in hand. Trusting God's timing requires us to remain steadfast, even in the face of uncertainty, knowing He is faithful to fulfill His promises.

Encouragement: Lamentations 3:25 – "The Lord is good to those whose hope is in Him, to the one who seeks Him."

Call to Action: As you embrace each day, commit to trusting God fully, waiting on Him patiently, and allowing Him to refine your character for His glory.

Reflection Questions
1. What areas of your life require more patience and trust in God?
2. How can you actively grow in faith while waiting on God's promises?
3. Who can you encourage with your testimony of God's faithfulness?

May these notes inspire you to deepen your walk with God as you embrace patience and faith daily!

J-14: Peace of Mind: Anchored in God's Presence

J-14: Prelude

The moment I submitted my resignation, I gained peace of mind—a blessing from God.

Defined: Peace of mind is a feeling of tranquility, calmness, and contentment that comes from being free of worry, stress, and anxiety.

Title: Peace of Mind: Anchored in God's Presence

Introduction

- Main Idea: True peace of mind is not found in external circumstances but in the presence of God. As we embrace each day, the assurance of God's sovereignty and love can guard our hearts and minds.

- Scripture Reference: Isaiah 26:3 – "You will keep in perfect peace those whose minds are steadfast, because they trust in You."

- Purpose: To explore how to attain and maintain peace of mind through God's Word, prayer, and trust in His promises.

Main Points
I. The Source of Peace

1. God as the Giver of Peace:
- Peace is a gift from God, not something the world can provide.
  - John 14:27 – "Peace I leave with you; My peace I give you. I do not give to you as the world gives. Do not let your hearts be troubled and do not be afraid."

2. Peace Through Reconciliation with God:
- True peace begins with a restored relationship with God through Jesus Christ.
  - Romans 5:1 – "Therefore, since we have been justified through faith, we have peace with God through our Lord Jesus Christ."

II. Obstacles to Peace of Mind

1. Anxiety and Worry:
- Worry consumes our thoughts and distracts us from trusting God.
  - Philippians 4:6-7 – "Do not be anxious about anything, but in every situation, by prayer and petition, with thanksgiving, present your requests to God. And the peace of God, which transcends all understanding, will guard your hearts and your minds in Christ Jesus."

2. Unresolved Sin:
- Guilt and shame disrupt our peace until we seek forgiveness.
  - 1 John 1:9 – "If we confess our sins, He is faithful and just and will forgive us our sins and purify us from all unrighteousness."

3. Distractions of the World:
- Materialism, busyness, and worldly pursuits can rob us of peace.
  - Mark 4:19 – "But the worries of this life, the deceitfulness of wealth and the desires for other things come in and choke the word, making it unfruitful."

III. Maintaining Peace of Mind

1. Trusting in God's Sovereignty:
- Trusting that God is in control brings calm in uncertain times.
  - Proverbs 3:5-6 – "Trust in the Lord with all your heart and lean not on your own understanding; in all your ways submit to Him, and He will make your paths straight."

2. Meditating on God's Word:
- Filling your mind with Scripture transforms your thoughts.
  - Psalm 119:165 – "Great peace have those who love Your law, and nothing can make them stumble."

3. Prayer as a Path to Peace:
- Regular prayer aligns our hearts with God's will.
  - 1 Peter 5:7 – "Cast all your anxiety on Him because He cares for you."

4. Being Spiritually Minded:
- A focus on spiritual things brings life and peace.
  - Romans 8:6 – "The mind governed by the flesh is death, but the mind governed by the Spirit is life and peace."

Application/Solutions
Practical Steps to Attain Peace of Mind:

1. Daily Quiet Time with God:
• Spend time in prayer and Scripture to center your thoughts.

2. Practice Gratitude:
• Thank God for His blessings, which shifts your focus from worry to trust.
   • 1 Thessalonians 5:18 – "Give thanks in all circumstances; for this is God's will for you in Christ Jesus."

3. Surrender Your Burdens:
• Let go of what you cannot control and place it in God's hands.

4. Surround Yourself with Godly Influence:
• Fellowship with believers who encourage you to stay grounded in faith.

5. Focus on Eternal Truths:
• Remember that God's promises are unchanging, even in a turbulent world.

Conclusion

• Summary: Peace of mind comes from trusting God, staying rooted in His Word, and surrendering life's worries to Him. It is a daily choice to focus on His presence and promises.

• Encouragement: Psalm 55:22 – "Cast your cares on the Lord and He will sustain you; He will never let the righteous be shaken."

• Call to Action: Embrace each day with the confidence that God is your peace. Commit to trusting Him fully and resting in His care, no matter what the year holds.

Reflection Questions

1. What areas of your life disrupt your peace of mind, and how can you surrender them to God?
2. How can you incorporate more prayer and Scripture meditation into your daily routine?
3. Who can you encourage with the peace that God has given you?

May these notes guide you to experience the true peace of mind that comes from God!

J-15: Overcoming Life's Tests: Embracing God's Strength

J-15: Prelude

Each of these journeys represents a life test I've personally experienced.

Title: Overcoming Life's Tests: Embracing God's Strength

Introduction

• Main Idea: Life is full of tests and trials, but with faith in God, we can overcome every challenge. These tests are opportunities for spiritual growth and proof of God's faithfulness.

• Scripture Reference: James 1:2-4 – "Consider it pure joy, my brothers and sisters, whenever you face trials of many kinds, because you know that the testing of your faith produces perseverance. Let perseverance finish its work so that you may be mature and complete, not lacking anything."

• Purpose: To encourage believers to approach life's tests with faith, trust in God, and perseverance, knowing He uses them to refine and strengthen us.

Main Points

I. Understanding Life's Tests

1. Purpose of Trials:

• Trials are not meant to harm us but to strengthen our faith.

  • 1 Peter 1:6-7 – "In all this you greatly rejoice, though now for a little while you may have had to suffer grief in all kinds of trials. These have come so that the proven genuineness of your faith—of greater worth than gold—may result in praise, glory, and honor when Jesus Christ is revealed."

2. Types of Tests:

• Financial struggles, health issues, relationship conflicts, career challenges, and spiritual doubts are some common tests.

• These tests reveal our character and dependence on God.

II. Biblical Examples of Overcoming Tests

1. Job: Faithfulness Amid Suffering
- Job faced loss of family, health, and possessions but remained steadfast in his faith.
  - Job 1:21 – "The Lord gave and the Lord has taken away; may the name of the Lord be praised."

2. Joseph: From the Pit to the Palace
- Joseph endured betrayal, slavery, and imprisonment but trusted God's plan.
  - Genesis 50:20 – "You intended to harm me, but God intended it for good to accomplish what is now being done, the saving of many lives."

3. Jesus: Overcoming Temptation
- Jesus overcame Satan's temptations in the wilderness by relying on God's Word.
  - Matthew 4:4 – "Man shall not live on bread alone, but on every word that comes from the mouth of God."

III. Strategies for Overcoming Life's Tests

1. Lean on God's Strength:
- Trust that God will provide the strength to endure.
  - Philippians 4:13 – "I can do all things through Christ who strengthens me."

2. Pray for Guidance and Wisdom:
- Ask God for clarity and strength during trials.
  - James 1:5 – "If any of you lacks wisdom, you should ask God, who gives generously to all without finding fault, and it will be given to you."

3. Stay Rooted in God's Word:
- Scripture is a source of comfort and direction during trials.
  - Psalm 119:105 – "Your word is a lamp for my feet, a light on my path."

4. Embrace Perseverance:
• View trials as opportunities for spiritual growth and maturity.
• Romans 5:3-5 – "Not only so, but we also glory in our sufferings, because we know that suffering produces perseverance; perseverance, character; and character, hope."

5. Rely on God's Promises:
• Hold onto the promises of God for peace and deliverance.
• Isaiah 41:10 – "So do not fear, for I am with you; do not be dismayed, for I am your God. I will strengthen you and help you; I will uphold you with My righteous right hand."

Application/Solutions
Practical Steps to Overcome Life's Tests:

1. Develop a Habit of Gratitude:
• Thank God even during trials, trusting His purpose.
• 1 Thessalonians 5:18 – "Give thanks in all circumstances; for this is God's will for you in Christ Jesus."

2. Build a Support System:
• Surround yourself with godly friends and mentors who encourage your faith.
• Ecclesiastes 4:9-10 – "Two are better than one... if either of them falls down, one can help the other up."

3. Remember Past Victories:
• Reflect on how God has helped you overcome past challenges.
• Psalm 77:11 – "I will remember the deeds of the Lord; yes, I will remember Your miracles of long ago."

4. Fix Your Eyes on Eternity:
• Life's tests are temporary; focus on the eternal rewards.
• 2 Corinthians 4:17 – "For our light and momentary troubles are achieving for us an eternal glory that far outweighs them all."

Conclusion

- Summary: Life's tests are inevitable, but we overcome them through faith, prayer, perseverance, and reliance on God's Word. They are tools for our growth and evidence of God's transformative power.

- Encouragement: John 16:33 – "In this world you will have trouble. But take heart! I have overcome the world."

- Call to Action: Embrace each day with confidence, knowing that God is with you in every test. Trust Him to turn trials into triumphs for His glory.

Reflection Questions

1. What tests are you currently facing, and how can you trust God to help you overcome them?
2. How has God used past trials to strengthen your faith?
3. Who can you encourage to overcome their tests through the truth of God's Word?

May these notes inspire you to approach life's tests with unwavering faith and hope!

J-16: Independent and Leaning into Friendship Circles

J-16: Prelude

Through life's lessons, I've learned not to place my faith entirely in others, as people inevitably let me down time and time again. Experiencing these disappointments shaped me into an independent woman who is cautious when selecting friends.

Friendships, I've realized, are either a reflection of who you are or a reflection of what you lack in your life. If you value friendships, you must accept that not everyone approaches them the way you do. Meeting people where they are is essential. That said, extreme independence can unintentionally push potential friends away by creating barriers, rejecting support, or avoiding vulnerability.

Despite this, I firmly believe in the principle of reciprocation. True friendships should reflect mutual care and effort, fostering a balanced and meaningful connection.

Title: Independent and Leaning into Friendship Circles

Introduction

- Main Idea: God designed us for community, even if we are naturally independent. Friendship circles provide support, encouragement, and accountability, helping us grow in faith and love. Balancing independence with meaningful relationships reflects God's intention for unity and fellowship.

- Scripture Reference: Ecclesiastes 4:9-10 – "Two are better than one, because they have a good return for their labor: If either of them falls down, one can help the other up."

- Purpose: To explore how Christians can cultivate friendships, embrace vulnerability, and grow in community while maintaining their unique independence.

Main Points

I. God's Design for Community

1. We Are Created for Relationship:
- From the beginning, God emphasized the importance of companionship.
  - Genesis 2:18 – "The Lord God said, 'It is not good for the man to be alone.'"

2. Jesus Modeled Community:
- Jesus surrounded Himself with friends and disciples, showing the value of fellowship.
  - John 15:15 – "I have called you friends, for everything that I learned from my Father I have made known to you."

3. The Early Church Thrived in Community:
- Believers in the early church shared life and faith together.
  - Acts 2:46-47 – "Every day they continued to meet together… They broke bread in their homes and ate together with glad and sincere hearts."

II. Balancing Independence with Community

1. Value Your God-Given Independence:
- Independence reflects confidence in your identity in Christ, but it must not lead to isolation.
  - Galatians 6:4-5 – "Each one should test their own actions... for each one should carry their own load."

2. Acknowledge the Need for Others:
- True strength comes from recognizing that others enrich and support our lives.
  - Proverbs 27:17 – "As iron sharpens iron, so one person sharpens another."

3. Leaning In Requires Vulnerability:
- Building meaningful friendships requires openness and trust.
  - James 5:16 – "Confess your sins to each other and pray for each other so that you may be healed."

III. Cultivating Healthy Friendship Circles

1. Seek Godly Relationships:
- Surround yourself with people who encourage your faith and walk with God.
  - 1 Corinthians 15:33 – "Do not be misled: 'Bad company corrupts good character.'"

2. Invest in Friendships:
- Deep relationships require time, effort, and mutual care.
  - Philippians 2:3-4 – "Do nothing out of selfish ambition... value others above yourselves, not looking to your own interests but each of you to the interests of the others."

3. Bear One Another's Burdens:
- True friendship involves supporting one another in times of need.

• Galatians 6:2 – "Carry each other's burdens, and in this way you will fulfill the law of Christ."

Application/Solutions
Practical Steps to Embrace Friendship Circles

1. Pray for God's Guidance in Relationships:
• Ask God to lead you to the right friends and to bless your efforts to connect.
• Psalm 37:23 – "The Lord makes firm the steps of the one who delights in him."

2. Engage in Church and Fellowship Groups:
• Participate in community activities to meet like-minded believers.
• Hebrews 10:24-25 – "Let us consider how we may spur one another on… not giving up meeting together."

3. Show Initiative and Gratitude:
• Be proactive in reaching out, and express appreciation for your friends.
• Proverbs 18:24 – "One who has unreliable friends soon comes to ruin, but there is a friend who sticks closer than a brother."

Conclusion

• Summary: Independence is a gift, but it is not a substitute for community. Leaning into friendship circles enriches our lives, strengthens our faith, and reflects God's design for relationship.

• Encouragement: As you seize each day, embrace the opportunities to build meaningful connections while remaining confident in your unique identity in Christ.

• Call to Action: Reflect on how you can balance your independence with the call to community. Take steps to foster deeper relationships in your friendship circles.

Reflection Questions

1. Are there areas of your life where you've prioritized independence over community?
2. How can you intentionally build stronger, Christ-centered friendships?
3. What steps can you take to become a better friend to those in your circle?

Commit to nurturing your relationships by leaning into friendship circles, fostering trust and care, and growing in community as God intended.

J-17: Letting Go of Strongholds: Finding Freedom in Christ

J-17: Prelude

I had grown accustomed to my strongholds, but letting them go, forced me to relearn how to live freely without their weight. Life has become lighter and more joyful, and the burdens I once carried no longer seem so heavy.

Title: Letting Go of Strongholds: Finding Freedom in Christ

Introduction

• Main Idea: Strongholds are spiritual barriers that hinder us from living in the fullness of God's purpose. They can be sins, negative thoughts, unhealthy habits, or deep fears. Through Christ, we are empowered to break free from every stronghold and walk in victory.

• Scripture Reference: 2 Corinthians 10:4-5 – "The weapons we fight with are not the weapons of the world. On the contrary, they have divine power to demolish strongholds."

• Purpose: To equip believers with the knowledge and tools to identify, confront, and demolish strongholds in their lives with renewed freedom and purpose.

Main Points

I. What Are Strongholds?

1. Definition of Strongholds:
• Spiritual strongholds are fortified places in our hearts and minds where lies, sin, or fear reign instead of God's truth.
  • Ephesians 4:27 – "Do not give the devil a foothold."

2. Examples of Strongholds:
• Fear (2 Timothy 1:7 – "For the Spirit God gave us does not make us timid, but gives us power, love, and self-discipline.")
• Unforgiveness (Matthew 6:14-15 – "If you do not forgive others, your Father will not forgive your sins.")
• Addictions, pride, negative self-perception, or recurring sin patterns.

II. Recognizing Strongholds in Your Life

1. Ask the Holy Spirit for Revelation:
• Prayerfully ask God to reveal areas of bondage or sin in your life.

- Psalm 139:23-24 – "Search me, God, and know my heart; test me and know my anxious thoughts. See if there is any offensive way in me, and lead me in the way everlasting."

2. Evaluate Your Thought Life:
- Strongholds often manifest as persistent negative or unbiblical thought patterns.
  - Proverbs 23:7 – "As a man thinks in his heart, so is he."

3. Assess Repeated Struggles:
- Patterns of behavior you cannot overcome on your own are often tied to strongholds.

III. Steps to Letting Go of Strongholds

1. Identify and Confess the Stronghold:
- Acknowledge the stronghold and repent of any sin associated with it.
  - 1 John 1:9 – "If we confess our sins, He is faithful and just and will forgive us our sins and purify us from all unrighteousness."

2. Renew Your Mind with God's Truth:
- Replace lies with the truth of Scripture.
  - Romans 12:2 – "Be transformed by the renewing of your mind."

3. Use Spiritual Weapons:
- Pray, fast, and declare God's Word to break strongholds.
  - Ephesians 6:17 – "Take the helmet of salvation and the sword of the Spirit, which is the word of God."

4. Rely on the Power of the Holy Spirit:
- True freedom comes from the Spirit's work in our lives.
  - Galatians 5:1 – "It is for freedom that Christ has set us free. Stand firm, then, and do not let yourselves be burdened again by a yoke of slavery."

5. Forgive and Release Others:
- Unforgiveness can be a stronghold that blocks your freedom.
  - Colossians 3:13 – "Forgive as the Lord forgave you."

IV. Walking in Freedom

1. Stay Rooted in God's Word:
- Continuously meditate on Scripture to reinforce your freedom.
  - Psalm 119:11 – "I have hidden Your word in my heart that I might not sin against You."

2. Remain Vigilant Against the Enemy:
- Satan will attempt to rebuild strongholds, but resist him through prayer and God's Word.
  - 1 Peter 5:8-9 – "Be alert and of sober mind. Your enemy the devil prowls around like a roaring lion looking for someone to devour. Resist him."

3. Seek Community and Accountability:
- Share your journey with trusted believers who can pray for and support you.
  - James 5:16 – "Confess your sins to each other and pray for each other so that you may be healed."

Application/Solutions
Living Free:

1. Daily Surrender: Begin each day by surrendering your thoughts, actions, and struggles to God.

2. Declare Victory in Christ: Speak life and freedom over yourself using Scriptures like Philippians 4:13 – "I can do all things through Christ who strengthens me."

3. Celebrate God's Faithfulness: Rejoice in the victories, big or small, and trust that God is completing His work in you.
- Philippians 1:6 – "He who began a good work in you will carry it on to completion."

Conclusion

- Summary: Strongholds are no match for the power of God. As you embrace each day, commit to identifying, confronting, and demolishing these barriers through faith, prayer, and God's Word.

- Encouragement: Freedom is possible, and God desires it for you! Trust Him to lead you into a life of victory and peace.

- Call to Action: John 8:36 – "If the Son sets you free, you will be free indeed." Walk in the freedom Christ has already secured for you!

Reflection Questions

1. What strongholds in your life need to be surrendered to God?
2. How can you use Scripture to renew your mind and overcome lies?
3. Who can you trust to support you in prayer and accountability on this journey?

May this be the year of breaking strongholds and walking boldly in the freedom and victory Christ has won for you!

J-18: Self-Love ♥: Embracing Your God-Given Worth

J-18: Prelude

Love yourself enough to want to change. Love yourself more. You can't truly love others—or God's people—until you first love yourself.

Title: Self-Love: Embracing Your God-Given Worth

Introduction

- Main Idea: Self-love is not selfish or sinful when it is rooted in recognizing your value as a creation of God. Loving yourself as God loves you enables you to live confidently, love others well, and fulfill your God-given purpose.

- Scripture Reference: Matthew 22:39 – "Love your neighbor as yourself."

- Purpose: To help believers understand the biblical foundation of self-love and cultivate a healthy self-image rooted in God's truth.

Main Points

I. What Is Self-Love According to the Bible?

1. Created in God's Image:
- Your worth is inherent because you are made in God's image.
  - Genesis 1:27 – "So God created mankind in His own image, in the image of God He created them."

2. God's Love Defines Your Value:
- God loved you so much He sent His Son to redeem you.
  - John 3:16 – "For God so loved the world that He gave His one and only Son."

3. Self-Love as a Foundation for Loving Others:
- Jesus commands us to love others as we love ourselves.
  - Ephesians 5:29 – "After all, no one ever hated their own body, but they feed and care for their body, just as Christ does the church."

II. The Dangers of Neglecting Self-Love

1. Unhealthy Self-Neglect:
• Ignoring your needs or living in self-hatred dishonors God's creation.
  • 1 Corinthians 6:19-20 – "Your body is a temple of the Holy Spirit... Therefore honor God with your body."

2. Burnout and Resentment:
• Pouring out without replenishing leads to emotional, physical, and spiritual exhaustion.
  • Mark 6:31 – "Come with Me by yourselves to a quiet place and get some rest."

3. Accepting Lies Over Truth:
• Believing negative labels or lies about yourself diminishes the power of God's truth in your life.
  • Psalm 139:14 – "I praise You because I am fearfully and wonderfully made."

III. Practicing Biblical Self-Love

1. See Yourself as God Sees You:
• Meditate on scriptures that affirm your worth in God's eyes.
  • Jeremiah 31:3 – "I have loved you with an everlasting love; I have drawn you with unfailing kindness."

2. Take Care of Your Physical and Mental Health:
• Self-care is stewardship of the body and mind God has given you.
  • 3 John 1:2 – "I pray that you may enjoy good health and that all may go well with you, even as your soul is getting along well."

3. Set Boundaries and Rest in God:
• Learning to say no and resting is essential to loving yourself.
  • Exodus 20:8 – "Remember the Sabbath day by keeping it holy."

IV. The Balance of Self-Love and Humility

1. Avoid Selfishness:
- Biblical self-love is not self-centered but rooted in honoring God and serving others.
  - Philippians 2:3-4 – "Do nothing out of selfish ambition or vain conceit. Rather, in humility value others above yourselves."

2. Glorify God Through Your Self-Love:
- Let your confidence in God's love reflect His glory.
  - Matthew 5:16 – "Let your light shine before others, that they may see your good deeds and glorify your Father in heaven."

3. Trust in God's Plan for You:
- Self-love is surrendering your identity to God and trusting Him.
  - Proverbs 3:5-6 – "Trust in the Lord with all your heart and lean not on your own understanding."

Application/Solutions
Living Out Self-Love

1. Daily Affirmation:
- Start each day by declaring God's truths over your life.
- Example: "I am loved, chosen, and purposed by God."

2. Invest in Your Well-Being:
- Make time for physical, emotional, and spiritual care.
  - 1 Timothy 4:8 – "For physical training is of some value, but godliness has value for all things."

3. Give and Receive Grace:
- Forgive yourself for past mistakes and walk in God's forgiveness.
  - Romans 8:1 – "There is now no condemnation for those who are in Christ Jesus."

4. Love Others Out of Abundance:
• The more you understand God's love for you, the better you can share it with others.
  • 1 John 4:19 – "We love because He first loved us."

Conclusion

• Summary: Biblical self-love is about recognizing your worth as God's creation and treating yourself with the care and respect that reflect His love for you. It's not about arrogance but about stewardship and gratitude.

• Encouragement: As you embrace each day, walk confidently in the knowledge that you are loved deeply by God. Let this truth empower you to love yourself well and love others effectively.

• Call to Action: Mark 12:30-31 – "Love the Lord your God with all your heart and with all your soul and with all your mind and with all your strength. The second is this: 'Love your neighbor as yourself.'"

Reflection Questions

1. How can you align your self-image with God's view of you?
2. What steps can you take to practice better self-care and stewardship?
3. How can loving yourself better enable you to love others more fully?

Begin each day by cultivating a God-centered self-love that empowers you to live purposefully and joyfully in His presence.

J-19: Understanding What a Blessing Is from God

J-19: Prelude

Do we truly understand what it means to receive "a blessing from God"? Have we begun to use the word "blessing" casually or take its significance for granted?

Title: Understanding What a Blessing Is from God

Introduction

- Main Idea: Many people equate blessings solely with material prosperity or comfort, but God's blessings encompass far more. They reflect His love, purpose, and provision in every area of life.

- Scripture Reference: James 1:17 – "Every good and perfect gift is from above, coming down from the Father of the heavenly lights, who does not change like shifting shadows."

- Purpose: To help believers discern and embrace God's blessings beyond material gains, recognizing His spiritual, emotional, and relational gifts as true treasures.

Main Points

I. Defining a Blessing from God

1. God's Goodness in Action:
- Blessings are tangible and intangible expressions of God's grace and favor.
  - Psalm 103:2-5 – "Praise the Lord, my soul, and forget not all His benefits."

2. Spiritual Over Material:
- Spiritual blessings, such as salvation and peace, are eternal, whereas material blessings are temporary.
  - Ephesians 1:3 – "Praise be to the God and Father of our Lord Jesus Christ, who has blessed us in the heavenly realms with every spiritual blessing in Christ."

II. Misconceptions About Blessings

1. Blessings Are Not Always Material Wealth:
- God's blessings can include trials that grow our faith and dependence on Him.
  - Romans 8:28 – "And we know that in all things God works for the good of those who love Him."

2. Blessings Are Not Earned:
- God's blessings are gifts of grace, not rewards for works.
  - Titus 3:5 – "He saved us, not because of righteous things we had done, but because of His mercy."

III. Types of Blessings from God

1. Spiritual Blessings:
- Salvation, forgiveness, the Holy Spirit, and eternal life.
  - John 3:16 – "For God so loved the world that He gave His one and only Son."

2. Relational Blessings:
- Family, friends, and community that reflect God's love.
  - Proverbs 17:17 – "A friend loves at all times, and a brother is born for a time of adversity."

3. Physical and Material Blessings:
- Health, provision, and safety, given as resources for God's purpose.
  - Matthew 6:33 – "But seek first His kingdom and His righteousness, and all these things will be given to you as well."

4. Blessings Through Trials:
- Difficult seasons that strengthen faith and refine character.
  - James 1:2-4 – "Consider it pure joy, my brothers and sisters, whenever you face trials of many kinds."

IV. How to Recognize God's Blessings

1. Stay Thankful in All Circumstances:
- Gratitude opens your eyes to see God's blessings, even in hardships.
  - 1 Thessalonians 5:18 – "Give thanks in all circumstances; for this is God's will for you in Christ Jesus."

2. Look Beyond the Surface:
• Seek God's purpose in every situation, understanding that blessings often come in disguise.
  • 2 Corinthians 4:17 – "For our light and momentary troubles are achieving for us an eternal glory that far outweighs them all."

3. Remain in Christ:
• Abiding in Jesus allows you to experience the fullness of God's blessings.
  • John 15:5 – "If you remain in Me and I in you, you will bear much fruit."

Application/Solutions
Living in the Reality of God's Blessings

1. Cultivate Gratitude Daily:
• Keep a journal of God's blessings to reflect on His faithfulness.
  • Psalm 118:24 – "This is the day that the Lord has made; let us rejoice and be glad in it."

2. Pray for Spiritual Discernment:
• Ask God for clarity to recognize His hand in every area of life.
  • Philippians 4:6-7 – "Do not be anxious about anything, but in every situation, by prayer and petition, with thanksgiving, present your requests to God."

3. Be a Blessing to Others:
• Share God's blessings by helping and encouraging others.
  • Acts 20:35 – "It is more blessed to give than to receive."

Conclusion
• Summary: Understanding blessings as more than material wealth helps believers live with deeper gratitude, contentment, and purpose. God's blessings are comprehensive, touching every part of our lives for His glory.

- Encouragement: Embrace each day with a heart that seeks and recognizes God's blessings in every circumstance, trusting in His perfect plan.

- Call to Action: Deuteronomy 28:2 – "All these blessings will come on you and accompany you if you obey the Lord your God."

Reflection Questions
1. How have you misunderstood God's blessings in the past?
2. What spiritual blessings can you thank God for today?
3. How can you become a blessing to someone else this week?

Commit to seeking God's blessings and sharing them generously with others, living as a testimony of His goodness.

J-20: The Trinity: God the Father, the Son & the Holy Spirit

J-20: Prelude

You must believe to receive!

Title: The Trinity: God the Father, the Son & the Holy Spirit

Introduction

- Main Idea: The Trinity is a foundational Christian doctrine that reveals God's nature as one Being in three distinct Persons: God the Father, God the Son (Jesus Christ), and God the Holy Spirit. Understanding the Trinity deepens our relationship with God and enriches our faith.

- Scripture Reference: Matthew 28:19 – "Therefore go and make disciples of all nations, baptizing them in the name of the Father and of the Son and of the Holy Spirit."

- Purpose: To explore the unity and distinct roles of the Trinity and its significance in our faith and daily walk with God.

Main Points

I. Understanding the Trinity: One God in Three Persons

1. The Oneness of God:
- Christianity is monotheistic—there is only one God.
  - Deuteronomy 6:4 – "Hear, O Israel: The Lord our God, the Lord is one."

2. Three Distinct Persons:
- The Father, Son, and Holy Spirit are distinct but coequal and coeternal.
  - John 1:1 – "In the beginning was the Word, and the Word was with God, and the Word was God."
  - 2 Corinthians 13:14 – "May the grace of the Lord Jesus Christ, and the love of God, and the fellowship of the Holy Spirit be with you all."

II. God the Father: Creator and Sustainer

1. Role in Creation and Sovereignty:
- The Father is the source of all creation and the sustainer of life.
  - Genesis 1:1 – "In the beginning God created the heavens and the earth."
  - Psalm 24:1 – "The earth is the Lord's, and everything in it."

2. Relationship with Humanity:
• God the Father is a loving and personal God.
  • Romans 8:15 – "The Spirit you received brought about your adoption to sonship. And by Him we cry, 'Abba, Father.'"

III. Jesus Christ: The Son and Savior

1. Role in Redemption:
• Jesus, fully God and fully man, came to save humanity from sin.
  • John 3:16 – "For God so loved the world that He gave His one and only Son."
  • 1 Timothy 2:5 – "For there is one God and one mediator between God and mankind, the man Christ Jesus."

2. Revealer of the Father:
• Jesus reveals the Father's heart and character.
  • John 14:9 – "Anyone who has seen Me has seen the Father."

IV. The Holy Spirit: Helper and Guide

1. Role in Empowerment:
• The Holy Spirit empowers believers to live a victorious Christian life.
  • Acts 1:8 – "But you will receive power when the Holy Spirit comes on you."
  • Galatians 5:22-23 – "But the fruit of the Spirit is love, joy, peace, forbearance, kindness, goodness, faithfulness, gentleness, and self-control."

2. Role in Guidance:
• The Holy Spirit leads believers into truth and convicts of sin.
  • John 16:13 – "But when He, the Spirit of truth, comes, He will guide you into all the truth."
  • Romans 8:26 – "The Spirit helps us in our weakness."

Application/Solutions
Living in the Reality of the Trinity

1. Worship God in Unity:
- Recognize and honor each Person of the Trinity in worship and prayer.
  - John 4:24 – "God is spirit, and His worshipers must worship in the Spirit and in truth."

2. Follow the Example of Jesus:
- Live in obedience to God's will, as Jesus did.
  - Philippians 2:5-8 – "In your relationships with one another, have the same mindset as Christ Jesus."

3. Walk in the Spirit:
- Rely on the Holy Spirit for daily guidance and strength.
  - Ephesians 5:18 – "Be filled with the Spirit."

Conclusion

- Summary: The Trinity reveals the fullness of God's love, grace, and power. God the Father creates, Jesus the Son redeems, and the Holy Spirit empowers and sustains.

- Encouragement: As you embrace each day, deepen your relationship with the Triune God by embracing the unique roles of the Father, Son, and Holy Spirit in your life.

- Call to Action: Reflect on the Trinity in your prayer life. Seek to know God in His fullness and allow Him to transform every area of your life.

Reflection Questions

1. How does understanding the Trinity impact your view of God?
2. In what ways can you grow in your relationship with God the Father, Jesus Christ, and the Holy Spirit?
3. How can you rely on the Holy Spirit more in your daily life?

Commit to living in unity with the Trinity, worshiping God fully, following Jesus faithfully, and walking in the Spirit daily.

J-21: What to Do When God Tells You to Move

J-21: Prelude

First, discern God's voice. Then, once confirmed, move without hesitation. Whatever God has for you will be great and perfect. Hallelujah!

Title: What to Do When God Tells You to Move

Introduction

- Main Idea: When God calls you to move—whether physically, spiritually, or emotionally—it can be daunting, but His plans are always for your good. Obedience to His guidance leads to blessings, growth, and fulfillment of His purposes.

- Scripture Reference: Genesis 12:1-2 – "The Lord had said to Abram, 'Go from your country, your people and your father's household to the land I will show you. I will make you into a great nation, and I will bless you.'"

- Purpose: To explore how to respond when God calls us to step out in faith and embrace the unknown.

Main Points
I. Recognizing God's Call to Move

1. God Speaks Through His Word:
- He confirms His direction through Scripture.
  - Psalm 119:105 – "Your word is a lamp for my feet, a light on my path."

2. God Speaks Through Circumstances:
- Sometimes He uses life changes to nudge us toward His will.
  - Proverbs 16:9 – "In their hearts humans plan their course, but the Lord establishes their steps."

3. God Speaks Through Prayer:
- Consistent prayer opens our hearts to hear His voice.
  - Jeremiah 33:3 – "Call to me and I will answer you and tell you great and unsearchable things you do not know."

II. Overcoming Fear and Doubt

1. Trust in God's Promises:
- Fear often arises from uncertainty, but God's plans are always good.
  - Jeremiah 29:11 – "For I know the plans I have for you," declares the Lord.

2. Rely on God's Strength:
- You don't move in your own power but in His.
  - Philippians 4:13 – "I can do all this through Him who gives me strength."

3. Remember God's Faithfulness:
- Reflect on past times He provided and guided you.
  - Deuteronomy 31:8 – "The Lord himself goes before you and will be with you."

III. Taking Practical Steps of Obedience

1. Seek Confirmation:
- Ask God for clarity and wisdom through prayer and counsel.
  - Proverbs 11:14 – "For lack of guidance a nation falls, but victory is won through many advisers."

2. Prepare for the Move:
- Practical preparation demonstrates trust and readiness.
  - Luke 14:28 – "Suppose one of you wants to build a tower. Won't you first sit down and estimate the cost to see if you have enough money to complete it?"

3. Step Out in Faith:
- God often reveals the next step, not the entire journey.
  - Hebrews 11:8 – "By faith Abraham, when called to go to a place he would later receive as his inheritance, obeyed and went, even though he did not know where he was going."

IV. Trusting God in the Transition

1. Stay Rooted in Prayer and Scripture:
• Prayer and God's Word keep you aligned with His will during uncertain times.
  • Joshua 1:8 – "Keep this Book of the Law always on your lips; meditate on it day and night."

2. Be Patient in the Process:
• God's timing is perfect, even if it feels slow.
  • Ecclesiastes 3:1 – "There is a time for everything, and a season for every activity under the heavens."

3. Expect Opposition:
• The enemy may try to discourage you, but stand firm in faith.
  • Ephesians 6:10-11 – "Be strong in the Lord and in His mighty power. Put on the full armor of God, so that you can take your stand against the devil's schemes."

Application/Solutions
Living Out the Move

1. Celebrate Small Victories:
• Recognize and thank God for progress along the way.
  • 1 Thessalonians 5:18 – "Give thanks in all circumstances."

2. Encourage Others to Obey God's Call:
• Share your journey to inspire others to trust Him.
  • Matthew 5:16 – "Let your light shine before others, that they may see your good deeds and glorify your Father in heaven."

3. Embrace Growth Through the Change:
• God uses every move to refine and mature us.
  • James 1:2-4 – "Consider it pure joy, my brothers and sisters, whenever you face trials of many kinds."

Conclusion

• Summary: When God tells you to move, it's an invitation to trust Him more deeply, step out in faith, and embrace the blessings He has prepared for you.

• Encouragement: Like Abraham, be willing to leave your comfort zone and trust that God's plan is greater than anything you could imagine.

• Call to Action: As you embrace each day, reflect on areas where God may be calling you to move—physically, spiritually, or emotionally. Take the first step of obedience and trust Him to lead the way.

Reflection Questions

1. Have you ever felt God prompting you to move? How did you respond?
2. What fears or doubts might be holding you back from obeying His call?
3. What practical steps can you take to prepare for God's direction in your life?

Say "yes" to God's call, trusting Him fully, and move forward in faith toward His purposes.

J-22: Heaven Revealed

J-22: Prelude

At times, I find myself wondering what heaven is truly like. As the Lord's Prayer says, *"Our Father, who art in heaven, hallowed be Thy name. Thy kingdom come, Thy will be done on earth as it is in heaven."* Could heaven already be here on earth? Might it exist within our hearts? Perhaps heaven is revealed in the fulfillment of God's will, both within us and through us.

Title: Heaven Revealed

Introduction

- Main Idea: Heaven is multifaceted within the Bible. It represents God's dwelling, a place of peace, love, worship, and the ultimate destination for those who are faithful to Him. Understanding the reality of heaven helps believers live in alignment with God's purpose and promises.

- Scripture Reference: Isaiah 66:1 – "This is what the Lord says: Heaven is my throne, and the earth is my footstool."

- Purpose: Revelation 21:4 – "He will wipe every tear from their eyes. There will be no more death or mourning or crying or pain."

Main Points

I. Heaven as God's Dwelling Place

1. Heaven is the Home of God:
- Heaven is primarily God's dwelling place where all things operate according to His will.
  - Psalm 103:19 – "The Lord has established His throne in heaven, and His kingdom rules over all."
- Heaven is not just a distant, ethereal realm but the very space where God reigns in His omniscience, omnipotence, and omnipresence.

2. Earth Reflects Heaven:
- As believers, we are living in God's presence and His heaven here on earth through our faith and connection with Him.
  - Matthew 6:10 – "Your kingdom come, Your will be done on earth as it is in heaven."
- Even though free will exists, God's will is always operative. When we call on Him, the Holy Spirit guides us, Jesus intercedes for us, and God works in alignment with His plans for our good.

3. Omniscience and Omnipresence:
- Omniscience Defined: possess all knowledge there is; knowing everything.
- Omnipresence Defined: being everywhere at once; constantly encountered.
- God's knowledge and presence remind us that even in moments of backsliding or doubt, He is always near, listening, and working.
  - Psalm 139:1-4 – "O Lord, You have searched me and known me... You are familiar with all my ways."

II. Heaven as a Place of Peace, Love, Worship, and Community

1. Peace, Love, Worship, and Unity:
- Heaven is described in the Bible as a place of eternal peace, love, worship, and perfect community among the redeemed.
  - Hebrews 12:14 – "Make every effort to live in peace with everyone and to be holy; without holiness no one will see the Lord."
- These qualities—peace, love, community—are not just future realities but can be experienced now when we live in relationship with God and His people.
- If these are cultivated in our hearts, then heaven is already alive within us.

2. No More Pain, Tears, or Sorrow:
- Heaven is a place free of suffering, sorrow, and pain. The old order of things will pass away.
  - Revelation 21:4 – "He will wipe every tear from their eyes. There will be no more death or mourning or crying or pain."
  - Matthew 11:28-30 – "Come to me, all you who are weary and burdened, and I will give you rest."

3. Death is Conquered:
- Believers have victory over death through rebirth in Jesus Christ.
  - John 11:25 – "Jesus said to her, 'I am the resurrection and the life. The one who believes in me will live, even though they die.'"
- Death is not the end but a transition into eternal life for those who trust in Jesus.

- Believers are called to die to self and allow the old life to be replaced with new life through Jesus.
- Galatians 2:20 – "I have been crucified with Christ and I no longer live, but Christ lives in me."

III. Living with the Hope of Heaven
Cultivating the Qualities of Heaven Here and Now:

1. Peace in the Midst of Trials:
- Even now, we can experience the peace of heaven through faith and trust.
- John 14:27 – "Peace I leave with you; my peace I give you."

2. Love for Others:
- Reflecting heavenly love by showing compassion, forgiveness, and grace.
- 1 John 4:7 – "Dear friends, let us love one another, for love comes from God."

3. Worship as a Way of Life:
- Worship is not just about attending church; it is a heart posture of reverence and gratitude.
- Romans 12:1 – "Offer your bodies as living sacrifices, holy and pleasing to God—this is your true and proper worship."

4. Looking Forward to Our Eternal Home:
- Heaven provides hope for all believers, offering the promise of eternal joy and reunion with God.
- Philippians 3:20-21 – "But our citizenship is in heaven. And we eagerly await a Savior from there, the Lord Jesus Christ."

Application/Solutions
1. When sorrow strikes, remember that the yoke of Jesus is light and His promises bring joy and peace to replace pain.
2. Live with the hope of heaven as a source of strength and motivation.

Conclusion

• Summary: Heaven is not just a distant reality but a place that represents God's presence, peace, and eternal promises. It is both a present reality for the believer (living in God's will and presence) and our eternal destination through faith in Jesus.

• Encouragement: As you embrace each day, let's commit to living with heavenly qualities now and maintaining hope in God's promise of eternal joy and restoration in heaven.

• Call to Action: Revelation 22:20 – "He who testifies to these things says, 'Yes, I am coming soon.' Amen. Come, Lord Jesus."

Reflection Questions

1. How can you better align your life with the peace, love, and community of heaven now?
2. In what ways can you trust in God's promises to replace your current pain, sorrow, or fear with His joy and peace?
3. How can you actively prepare your heart for the hope of heaven?

Let's live each day with heaven in mind—reflecting peace, love, and worship as we trust God's plan and await His return.

J-23: Renew Mindset or Self-Sabotage

J-23: Prelude

Our mindset plays a crucial role in our daily lives. What we feel shapes our thoughts, and those thoughts drive our actions. On my journey, I realized that I needed to remove "stinking thinking"—negative, self-sabotaging thoughts that kept me stagnant and trapped in my comfort zone. Letting go of these patterns has allowed me to grow, and I've come to deeply appreciate this process of renewal.

Title: Renew Mindset or Self-Sabotage

Introduction

- Main Idea: Begin with the question: How fully does the Lord dwell within you? Is your behavior in line with God's will? Aligning yourself, your thoughts, your beliefs with God's perspective effectively prevents self-sabotage.

Scripture Reference: Romans 12:2, "Do not conform to the pattern of this world, but be transformed by the renewing of your mind. Then you will be able to test and approve what God's will is--his good, pleasing nd perfect will."

- Purpose: To reflect on the depth and strength of your relationship with God. Is His presence evident in your life?

I. Illustration: A Physical Example

- Invite three people to stand side by side, holding hands.
- The person in the middle represents YOU.
- The people on either side represent those God has placed in your life to support you in your walk—this could include a spiritual group, prayer partners, friends, family, or even God's Word itself.

II. The Role of Godly Support

- These individuals represent vessels through which God speaks and works in your life.
  - Philippians 2:13, "God works in people to will and act in order to fulfill his good purpose."
- They pour God's Word into you, encourage you, call out your missteps, and celebrate your growth.
- God places them in your life to guide and strengthen your journey.
  - Declare together: "Greater is He that is in me."

III. How We Can Dampen the "Greater"

- Sometimes, we hinder God's work in us through disobedience, doubt, or distraction.
- Illustration Example: Have the person in the middle squat down while the others remain standing and all try to walk together.
- This represents how we make our walk with God a struggle when we resist His Word or blame others for our own choices.

IV. The "Sometimey" Relationship

- When we're inconsistent in our relationship with God, our connection to Him weakens.
- Sometimes, we're receptive to His Word; other times, the message is unclear or ignored.
- This inconsistent walk reflects a lack of spiritual stability.

V. The Power of Standing Firm

- Illustration Example: Encourage the person in the middle to stand up tall and firm.
- When you take action over your life, aligning yourself with God's will, you strengthen your walk.
  - Philippians 4:13, "I can do all things through Christ who strengthens me."
- Illustration Example: Have all three individuals walk together now, showing how unity and alignment with God bring clarity, strength, and peace.

VI. A Renewed Walk with God

- When you stand firm, you position yourself to better hear, understand, and receive God's Word.
  - Proverb 16:9, "The heart of man plans his way, but the Lord establishes his steps."
- Your walk becomes less of a struggle, and you are better equipped to fulfill His purpose in your life.

VII. Declare God's Greatness

- Together, proclaim: "Greater is He that is in me."
- Remind yourself and others: If much of God is in you, His greatness will shine through you for all to see.
  - Psalms 145:21, "My mouth will speak in praise of the Lord. Let every creature praise his holy name for ever and ever."

Application/Solutions

- Evaluate your relationship with God today. Does your mind honor Christ or does your mind chase after pleasure, possessions or status?
- Commit to work towards God's perfect will so that you can achieve true success.

Conclusion

- To God be the glory! And that glory must come from you.
- Glorify Him by living a life that reflects His presence and power within you.
- "Greater is He that is in me" isn't just a statement—it's a way of life.

If you allow God's fullness to dwell in you, others will see His light through you, and your life will glorify Him. But if you resist, the world will see less of Him and more of the struggle. Choose today to embrace His greatness and stand firm in faith.

J-24: What to Do When You Can't Distinguish God's Voice

J-24: Prelude

As I mentioned in J-12, I initially struggled to discern God's voice, which led to disobedience and another wrestle with the Holy Spirit. Naturally, I lost. But when I listened the second time, I experienced true victory.

Title: What to Do When You Can't Distinguish God's Voice

Introduction

• Main Idea: At times, hearing God's voice may feel challenging, but God promises to guide His children. Through His Word, prayer, and the Holy Spirit, He provides clarity to those who diligently seek Him.

• Scripture Reference: John 10:27 – "My sheep listen to my voice; I know them, and they follow me."

• Purpose: To explore practical and spiritual steps to discern God's voice in times of confusion.

Main Points

I. Why God's Voice May Seem Hard to Distinguish

1. Spiritual Interference:
• Unconfessed sin can create distance.
  • Isaiah 59:2 – "But your iniquities have separated you from your God."
• The enemy seeks to confuse and distract.
  • 1 Peter 5:8 – "Be alert and of sober mind. Your enemy the devil prowls around like a roaring lion."

2. Busyness and Noise:
• The chaos of life can drown out God's still, small voice.
  • Psalm 46:10 – "Be still, and know that I am God."

3. God's Silence as a Test:
• Sometimes, God uses silence to deepen faith.
  • Deuteronomy 8:2 – "...to humble and test you in order to know what was in your heart."

II. Steps to Recognize God's Voice

1. Study the Scriptures:
• God primarily speaks through His Word.
  • 2 Timothy 3:16-17 – "All Scripture is God-breathed and is useful for teaching, rebuking, correcting, and training in righteousness."

2. Pray with Expectation:
• Prayer opens the heart to God's guidance.
  • Jeremiah 33:3 – "Call to me and I will answer you and tell you great and unsearchable things you do not know."

3. Listen to the Holy Spirit:
• The Holy Spirit provides clarity and conviction.
  • John 16:13 – "But when he, the Spirit of truth, comes, he will guide you into all the truth."

4. Seek Godly Counsel:
• Wise counsel can affirm God's direction.
  • Proverbs 15:22 – "Plans fail for lack of counsel, but with many advisers they succeed."

III. Overcoming Doubt and Confusion

1. Trust God's Character:
• He desires to guide His children for their good.
  • Jeremiah 29:11 – "For I know the plans I have for you, declares the Lord."

2. Surrender to His Will:
• Yielding to God's plan clears the path for clarity.
  • Proverbs 3:5-6 – "Trust in the Lord with all your heart and lean not on your own understanding."

3. Practice Patience:
• God's timing is perfect; don't rush the process.
   • Ecclesiastes 3:1 – "There is a time for everything, and a season for every activity under the heavens."

Application/Solutions
Living Out Discernment

1. Regularly Quiet Your Heart:
• Create space for God by eliminating distractions.
   • Mark 1:35 – "Very early in the morning, while it was still dark, Jesus got up, left the house and went off to a solitary place, where he prayed."

2. Document What You Sense:
• Write down thoughts, impressions, and Scriptures.
   • Habakkuk 2:2 – "Write down the revelation and make it plain on tablets."

3. Step Forward in Faith:
• Take small, obedient steps, trusting God to reveal the next.
   • Hebrews 11:6 – "And without faith it is impossible to please God."

Conclusion

• Summary: Discerning God's voice requires a heart tuned to Him through Scripture, prayer, and trust. Even in silence, He is working to draw you closer and guide your steps.

• Encouragement: God's voice may not always be loud, but it is always present. Lean into His Word and His Spirit, trusting that He will reveal His will in His perfect time.

• Call to Action: As you embrace each day, commit to deepening your relationship with God. Remove distractions, immerse yourself in His Word, and practice stillness to hear Him clearly.

Reflection Questions

1. Are there distractions in your life hindering you from hearing God's voice?
2. How can you incorporate more stillness and Scripture into your daily routine?
3. Who can you seek for godly counsel to help discern God's will?

Make it your goal to distinguish God's voice with confidence by prioritizing His Word, staying rooted in prayer, and trusting His guidance every step of the way.

J-25: Experiencing a Loss: Finding God in Grief

J-25: Prelude

Experiencing loss in any form is never easy. Through my own struggles with loss, I've come to realize how deeply I need God—literally, spiritually, and physically.

Title: Experiencing a Loss: Finding God in Grief

Introduction

- Main Idea: Loss is an inevitable part of life, but God offers comfort, healing, and hope through His Word and presence. In times of grief, we can lean on His promises and experience His peace.

- Scripture Reference: Psalm 34:18 – "The Lord is close to the brokenhearted and saves those who are crushed in spirit."

- Purpose: To provide biblical principles and practical steps to process grief, find comfort in God, and move toward healing.

Main Points

I. Understanding Grief Through a Biblical Lens

1. Grief is a Natural Response to Loss:
- Even Jesus grieved when He lost loved ones.
  - John 11:35 – "Jesus wept."

2. God is Present in Our Pain:
- He never abandons us, even in our darkest moments.
  - Deuteronomy 31:8 – "The Lord himself goes before you and will be with you; he will never leave you nor forsake you."

3. Grief Has a Purpose:
- God uses grief to draw us closer to Him and refine our faith.
  - Romans 8:28 – "And we know that in all things God works for the good of those who love him."

II. Finding Comfort in God During Loss

1. Seek God's Presence:
- His presence brings peace and reassurance.
  - Matthew 5:4 – "Blessed are those who mourn, for they will be comforted."

2. Pour Out Your Heart to God:
• Prayer is a safe space to express your pain and sorrow.
  • Psalm 62:8 – "Trust in him at all times, you people; pour out your hearts to him, for God is our refuge."

3. Lean on God's Promises:
• His Word reminds us of His love and eternal hope.
  • Isaiah 41:10 – "Do not fear, for I am with you; do not be dismayed, for I am your God. I will strengthen you and help you."

III. Moving Toward Healing and Hope

1. Allow Yourself to Grieve:
• Grief is a journey, not a destination; take time to process.
  • Ecclesiastes 3:1, 4 – "There is a time for everything… a time to weep and a time to laugh, a time to mourn and a time to dance."

2. Find Community and Support:
• Share your grief with others who can provide encouragement.
  • Galatians 6:2 – "Carry each other's burdens, and in this way you will fulfill the law of Christ."

3. Trust in God's Eternal Plan:
• Loss on earth is temporary; eternal life awaits in heaven.
  • Revelation 21:4 – "He will wipe every tear from their eyes. There will be no more death or mourning or crying or pain."

Application/Solutions
Living Out Faith Through Loss

1. Anchor Yourself in God's Word:
• Daily Scripture reading provides strength and perspective.
  • Psalm 119:50 – "My comfort in my suffering is this: Your promise preserves my life."

2. Seek Comfort in Worship:
• Worship shifts our focus from pain to God's goodness.
  • Isaiah 61:3 – "...to bestow on them a crown of beauty instead of ashes, the oil of joy instead of mourning."

3. Help Others Who Are Grieving:
• Serving others in their pain can bring healing to your own heart.
  • 2 Corinthians 1:3-4 – "God comforts us in all our troubles, so that we can comfort those in any trouble with the comfort we ourselves receive from God."

Conclusion

• Summary: Loss is a difficult but transformative experience that allows us to draw closer to God. Through His Word, His presence, and the support of others, we can find healing and hope in Him.

• Encouragement: Remember that grief is not the end of the story. God offers comfort now and promises eternal joy in His presence.

• Call to Action: As you embrace each day, commit to trusting God through your grief and allowing Him to heal your heart.

Reflection Questions

1. How have you experienced God's comfort in times of loss?
2. What Scriptures or promises of God bring you the most peace in difficult times?
3. How can you support someone in your life who is grieving?

Resolve to seek God's peace and comfort in every season of loss, trusting Him to bring beauty from ashes and joy from sorrow.

J-26: In Silence Comes Wisdom

J-26: Prelude

With so many external and internal factors, our minds are constantly on the move. Quieting the mind and resisting the urge to always have an opinion is a challenging task. So, how do I gain wisdom in being silent?

Title: In Silence Comes Wisdom

Introduction

• Main Idea: In a world full of noise and distractions, silence creates space for God's voice to be heard and wisdom to be cultivated. Through intentional stillness, we allow God's wisdom to shape our thoughts, actions, and understanding.

• Scripture Reference: Proverbs 17:28 – "Even fools are thought wise if they keep silent, and discerning if they hold their tongues."

• Purpose: To explore the power of silence in seeking God's wisdom and how it leads to a deeper relationship with Him and others.

Main Points
I. The Biblical Call to Silence

1. Silence Honors God's Presence:
• Silence allows us to reflect on God's greatness and listen for His guidance.
  • Habakkuk 2:20 – "The Lord is in his holy temple; let all the earth be silent before him."

2. Silence Precedes Understanding:
• Wisdom often comes when we stop talking and start listening.
  • Ecclesiastes 3:7 – "A time to be silent and a time to speak."

3. Jesus Modeled Silence:
• In times of decision or trial, Jesus embraced silence to connect with God.
  • Matthew 14:23 – "After he had dismissed them, he went up on a mountainside by himself to pray. Later that night, he was there alone."

II. The Benefits of Silence in Gaining Wisdom

1. Silence Enables Listening to God:
• Wisdom begins with hearing God's voice, which often requires quieting our own.
  • Psalm 46:10 – "Be still, and know that I am God."

2. Silence Guards Against Foolishness:
• Speaking too quickly can lead to errors; silence fosters thoughtfulness.
  • Proverbs 10:19 – "Sin is not ended by multiplying words, but the prudent hold their tongues."

3. Silence Strengthens Discernment:
• Through silence, we can process situations and respond wisely.
  • James 1:19 – "Everyone should be quick to listen, slow to speak and slow to become angry."

III. Practicing Silence to Grow in Wisdom

1. Set Aside Time for Stillness:
• Create intentional moments of quiet to hear from God.
  • Mark 1:35 – "Very early in the morning, while it was still dark, Jesus got up, left the house and went off to a solitary place, where he prayed."

2. Meditate on God's Word:
• Silence your heart to reflect deeply on Scripture.
  • Joshua 1:8 – "Keep this Book of the Law always on your lips; meditate on it day and night."

3. Practice Restraint in Conversations:
• Choose words carefully, and listen more than you speak.
  • Proverbs 13:3 – "Those who guard their lips preserve their lives, but those who speak rashly will come to ruin."

Application/Solutions
Living Out Silence for Wisdom

1. Develop a Habit of Daily Quiet Time:
- Spend time alone with God to align your heart with His wisdom.
  - Psalm 37:7 – "Be still before the Lord and wait patiently for him."

2. Seek God's Guidance Before Acting:
- Pause to seek clarity and wisdom in decision-making.
  - Isaiah 30:21 – "Whether you turn to the right or to the left, your ears will hear a voice behind you, saying, 'This is the way; walk in it.'"

3. Use Silence to Reflect and Grow Spiritually:
- Let silence become a tool for examining your heart and seeking God's will.
  - Lamentations 3:26 – "It is good to wait quietly for the salvation of the Lord."

Conclusion

- Summary: Silence is a sacred tool for cultivating wisdom and drawing closer to God. By choosing to pause and reflect, we allow God's wisdom to shape our words, thoughts, and actions.

- Encouragement: As you embrace each day, make a habit of practicing intentional silence to hear God's voice and gain clarity for the journey ahead.

- Call to Action: Commit to daily moments of stillness, whether through prayer, meditation, or quiet reflection, and watch how God's wisdom flows into your life.

Reflection Questions
1. How can you create more space for silence in your daily life?
2. What distractions keep you from hearing God's voice clearly?
3. How has silence helped you make wise decisions in the past?

Resolve to embrace silence as a means to grow in wisdom and deepen your connection with God, trusting that His voice will guide you in every decision.

J-27: Nourishing Your Needs

J-27: Prelude

For so long, I placed myself on the back burner, always prioritizing others over my own needs. I devoted myself to ensuring the happiness of my husband, children, parents, siblings, extended family, and friends, often neglecting my own well-being. Early in my marriage, I told my husband, "I have to take care of my family." I carried the weight of being the "strong one," which often meant putting myself last.

Over time, I realized that the love and care I poured into others weren't being reciprocated. The more I gave, the more they took. In my efforts to ensure everyone else's joy, I had completely forgotten about my own. That's when I made the decision to take a stand for myself. I chose to be "selfish"—not in a negative way, but by learning to love and prioritize myself so that I could pour into others from a place of fullness.

Title: Nourishing Your Needs

Introduction

• Main Idea: God designed us with physical, emotional, and spiritual needs, and He provides the resources to nourish them. By seeking Him and applying His Word, we can find fulfillment and strength in every area of life.

• Scripture Reference: Philippians 4:19 – "And my God will meet all your needs according to the riches of his glory in Christ Jesus."

• Purpose: To understand how God meets our needs and how we can actively nourish ourselves through His provisions and principles.

Main Points
I. Recognizing the Source of Nourishment

1. God is the Ultimate Provider:
• All our needs—physical, emotional, and spiritual—are met by God.
 • Psalm 23:1 – "The Lord is my shepherd; I lack nothing."

2. Jesus as the Bread of Life:
• Christ nourishes our souls and sustains us eternally.
 • John 6:35 – "Then Jesus declared, 'I am the bread of life. Whoever comes to me will never go hungry, and whoever believes in me will never be thirsty.'"

3. The Holy Spirit as Living Water:
• The Spirit refreshes and fills us with God's presence.
 • John 7:38-39 – "Whoever believes in me, as Scripture has said, rivers of living water will flow from within them."

II. Identifying and Addressing Our Needs

1. Physical Needs:
- God provides for our physical well-being, but we must care for our bodies.
  - 1 Corinthians 6:19-20 – "Do you not know that your bodies are temples of the Holy Spirit...?"

2. Emotional Needs:
- God gives peace, joy, and comfort to sustain our emotions.
  - Matthew 11:28-30 – "Come to me, all you who are weary and burdened, and I will give you rest."

3. Spiritual Needs:
- Regular communion with God nourishes our spirits.
  - Matthew 4:4 – "Man shall not live on bread alone, but on every word that comes from the mouth of God."

III. Nourishing Yourself Through God's Provision

1. Engage in Prayer:
- Prayer connects us to God's wisdom and peace.
  - Philippians 4:6-7 – "Do not be anxious about anything, but in every situation...present your requests to God."

2. Meditate on Scripture:
- The Word nourishes and strengthens our inner being.
  - Joshua 1:8 – "Keep this Book of the Law always on your lips; meditate on it day and night."

3. Fellowship with Believers:
- Community strengthens and supports us in our journey.
  - Hebrews 10:24-25 – "Let us consider how we may spur one another on...not giving up meeting together."

4. Practice Rest and Sabbath:
• Rest is essential for renewal and alignment with God.
• Exodus 20:8 – "Remember the Sabbath day by keeping it holy."

Application/Solutions
Living a Nourished Life

1. Set Daily Spiritual Habits:
• Start your day with prayer and Scripture to nourish your spirit.
  • Psalm 119:105 – "Your word is a lamp for my feet, a light on my path."

2. Prioritize Self-Care:
• Care for your physical and emotional well-being as part of honoring God.
  • 3 John 1:2 – "I pray that you may enjoy good health and that all may go well with you."

3. Seek God for Every Need:
• Trust Him to meet your needs, even in times of lack.
  • Matthew 6:33 – "Seek first his kingdom and his righteousness, and all these things will be given to you as well."

Conclusion

• Summary: God provides for every aspect of our lives, and we are called to nourish ourselves through His provisions. By focusing on prayer, Scripture, rest, and fellowship, we can experience His fullness.

• Encouragement: As you embrace each day, remember that God cares about every need in your life. Trust Him to provide and take intentional steps to nourish your mind, body, and spirit.

• Call to Action: Identify one area of your life—physical, emotional, or spiritual—that needs nourishment, and commit to a plan of action to address it with God's help.

Reflection Questions

1. What areas of your life need more nourishment—physically, emotionally, or spiritually?
2. How can you better rely on God's provision for your needs?
3. What steps can you take to nourish your relationship with God?

Commit to nourishing yourself through prayer, Scripture, rest, and community, trusting that God will provide abundantly for all your needs.

J-28: Discovering Your Path

J-28: Prelude

None of us know exactly what God has for us. We move forward with hope, faith, and prayer, trusting that we are aligned with His will. If we knew the exact day and hour of His plans, we might try to take matters into our own hands—attempting to play God.

Title: Discovering Your Path

Introduction

- Main Idea: Discovering your God-ordained path requires seeking Him wholeheartedly, understanding His purpose for your life, and walking in faith. God has a unique plan for each person, and following His direction brings fulfillment and peace.

- Scripture Reference: Proverbs 3:5-6 – "Trust in the Lord with all your heart and lean not on your own understanding; in all your ways submit to Him, and He will make your paths straight."

- Purpose: To equip believers with practical steps to discern and follow the path God has designed for their lives.

Main Points

I. Understanding God's Purpose for Your Life

1. God Created You with Purpose:
- Every person has been uniquely designed for a specific calling.
  - Jeremiah 29:11 – "For I know the plans I have for you," declares the Lord, "plans to prosper you and not to harm you, plans to give you hope and a future."

2. God's Purpose Brings Fulfillment:
- True contentment comes from walking in alignment with God's will.
  - Psalm 37:4 – "Take delight in the Lord, and He will give you the desires of your heart."

3. God's Plan Glorifies Him:
- Your path is designed to bring glory to God and impact others.
  - Matthew 5:16 – "Let your light shine before others, that they may see your good deeds and glorify your Father in heaven."

II. Seeking God's Guidance for Your Path

1. Through Prayer:
- Consistent communication with God reveals His direction.
  - James 1:5 – "If any of you lacks wisdom, you should ask God, who gives generously to all without finding fault, and it will be given to you."

2. Through Scripture:
- The Word is a lamp that illuminates our path.
  - Psalm 119:105 – "Your word is a lamp for my feet, a light on my path."

3. Through the Holy Spirit:
- The Spirit provides guidance and wisdom in decision-making.
  - John 16:13 – "But when He, the Spirit of truth, comes, He will guide you into all the truth."

4. Through Wise Counsel:
- Seek advice from godly mentors and fellow believers.
  - Proverbs 15:22 – "Plans fail for lack of counsel, but with many advisers they succeed."

III. Overcoming Challenges on the Journey

1. Overcome Fear and Doubt:
- Trust God's promises when the path feels uncertain.
  - Isaiah 41:10 – "Do not fear, for I am with you; do not be dismayed, for I am your God."

2. Be Patient in the Process:
- God's timing is perfect, even if it feels delayed.
- Ecclesiastes 3:1 – "There is a time for everything, and a season for every activity under the heavens."

3. Stand Firm Against Opposition:
- The enemy may try to discourage you, but God is greater.
  - Ephesians 6:10-11 – "Be strong in the Lord and in His mighty power. Put on the full armor of God."

IV. Walking in Faith

1. Take Small Steps of Obedience:
- Even small acts of faith lead to greater clarity.
  - Hebrews 11:8 – "By faith Abraham, when called to go to a place he would later receive as his inheritance, obeyed and went."

2. Stay Rooted in God's Promises:
- Meditate on His Word for strength and encouragement.
  - Joshua 1:9 – "Have I not commanded you? Be strong and courageous."

3. Trust God for the Outcome:
- Surrender the results to God and remain faithful.
  - Romans 8:28 – "And we know that in all things God works for the good of those who love Him."

Application/Solutions
Living Out Your Path

1. Dedicate Time to God Daily:
- Invest in prayer, Bible study, and quiet reflection.
  - Matthew 6:33 – "Seek first His kingdom and His righteousness, and all these things will be given to you as well."

2. Set God-Centered Goals:
- Write down practical steps to align your life with God's purpose.
  - Habakkuk 2:2 – "Write down the revelation and make it plain on tablets so that a herald may run with it."

3. Embrace Growth Through Challenges:
- Trust that trials shape you for the journey ahead.
  - James 1:2-4 – "Consider it pure joy...whenever you face trials of many kinds."

Conclusion

• Summary: Discovering your path is a journey of trust, patience, and faith. As you seek God through prayer, Scripture, and the guidance of the Holy Spirit, He will reveal His purpose for your life.

• Encouragement: Trust that God's plan is perfect, and even when the way is unclear, He is walking with you. Your path is unique, and He will equip you for every step.

• Call to Action: Commit to seeking God daily for direction and take the first step of faith in discovering the path He has designed for you.

Reflection Questions

1. Are you actively seeking God's guidance for your life's path?
2. What steps can you take to better align your life with His purpose?
3. How can you trust God more in seasons of uncertainty?

Resolve to discover and walk in God's path for your life, trusting His wisdom, timing, and provision as you move forward in faith.

J-29: Spiritual Evolution: Growing in Faith & Maturity

J-29: Prelude

Reading God's Word has helped me grow spiritually. It's hard to put into words, but let me give an example. My insight has improved. I've always been a praying woman, but the way I pray has changed. I'm more intentional and vocal about sharing God's Word, though I prefer one-on-one or small-group settings. I strive to see from the spiritual perspective rather than through the lens of the flesh. Still, I'm a work in progress. Sometimes I catch myself before I go astray—or I reel myself back when I do.

Title: Spiritual Evolution: Growing in Faith & Maturity

Introduction

• Main Idea: Spiritual evolution is the process of growing deeper in your relationship with God, maturing in faith, and being transformed into the image of Christ. It requires intentional effort, divine guidance, and a commitment to becoming more like Jesus.

• Scripture Reference: 2 Corinthians 3:18 – "And we all, who with unveiled faces contemplate the Lord's glory, are being transformed into His image with ever-increasing glory, which comes from the Lord, who is the Spirit."

• Purpose: To understand the process of spiritual growth and encourage believers to actively pursue transformation in Christ as they prepare for the new year.

Main Points

I. The Foundation of Spiritual Evolution

1. Understanding Salvation as the Starting Point:
• Spiritual growth begins with accepting Jesus Christ as Lord and Savior.
 • Ephesians 2:8-9 – "For it is by grace you have been saved, through faith—and this is not from yourselves, it is the gift of God—not by works, so that no one can boast."

2. Recognizing the Role of the Holy Spirit:
• The Holy Spirit empowers and guides believers in their transformation.
 • John 14:26 – "But the Advocate, the Holy Spirit, whom the Father will send in my name, will teach you all things and will remind you of everything I have said to you."

3. Anchoring in God's Word:
- Growth is fueled by regular engagement with Scripture.
  - Psalm 1:2-3 – "But whose delight is in the law of the Lord, and who meditates on His law day and night. That person is like a tree planted by streams of water."

II. The Process of Spiritual Evolution

1. Developing Spiritual Disciplines:
- Practices such as prayer, fasting, and worship deepen intimacy with God.
  - Matthew 6:6 – "But when you pray, go into your room, close the door and pray to your Father, who is unseen."

2. Embracing Transformation Through Renewal:
- True growth requires a renewal of the mind and heart.
  - Romans 12:2 – "Do not conform to the pattern of this world, but be transformed by the renewing of your mind."

3. Learning Through Trials:
- Challenges refine faith and develop perseverance.
  - James 1:2-4 – "Consider it pure joy, my brothers and sisters, whenever you face trials of many kinds, because you know that the testing of your faith produces perseverance."

4. Bearing Spiritual Fruit:
- Growth is evident through the fruits of the Spirit in your life.
  - Galatians 5:22-23 – "But the fruit of the Spirit is love, joy, peace, forbearance, kindness, goodness, faithfulness, gentleness, and self-control."

III. Obstacles to Spiritual Evolution

1. Complacency and Lack of Hunger for Growth:
- Overcoming spiritual stagnation requires diligence.
  - Hebrews 5:12-14 – "In fact, though by this time you ought to be teachers, you need someone to teach you the elementary truths of God's word all over again."

3. Fear of Change:
- Trusting God's plan overcomes fear of transformation.
  - Isaiah 41:10 – "So do not fear, for I am with you; do not be dismayed, for I am your God."

IV. Steps to Accelerate Spiritual Evolution

1. Commit to Daily Spiritual Practices:
- Consistency in prayer, study, and worship leads to steady growth.
  - Joshua 1:8 – "Keep this Book of the Law always on your lips; meditate on it day and night."

2. Seek Accountability and Fellowship:
- Growing with others fosters encouragement and accountability.
  - Proverbs 27:17 – "As iron sharpens iron, so one person sharpens another."

3. Live Out Your Faith Boldly:
- Sharing the gospel and serving others help refine and strengthen faith.
  - Matthew 5:16 – "Let your light shine before others, that they may see your good deeds and glorify your Father in heaven."

Application/Solutions
Living Out Spiritual Evolution

1. Set Spiritual Goals for Growth:
- Identify areas in your life where you desire to grow spiritually.
  - Habakkuk 2:2 – "Write down the revelation and make it plain on tablets so that a herald may run with it."

2. Regularly Examine Your Heart:
- Ask God to reveal areas needing growth and refinement.
  - Psalm 139:23-24 – "Search me, God, and know my heart; test me and know my anxious thoughts."

3. Celebrate Progress in Your Journey:
• Rejoice in small victories as evidence of God's work in you.
  • Philippians 1:6 – "Being confident of this, that He who began a good work in you will carry it on to completion."

Conclusion

• Summary: Spiritual evolution is a continuous journey of becoming more like Christ through intentional growth, reliance on the Holy Spirit, and perseverance through challenges.

• Encouragement: God is faithful to complete the work He has begun in you. Trust His timing and embrace the transformation process.

• Call to Action: As you embrace each day, commit to growing spiritually by deepening your relationship with God, overcoming obstacles, and bearing fruit for His glory.

Reflection Questions

1. What areas of your spiritual life need intentional growth?
2. How can you incorporate spiritual disciplines into your daily routine?
3. Who can you partner with for accountability in your spiritual journey?

Resolve to embrace spiritual evolution by seeking God wholeheartedly, committing to growth, and becoming the person He has created you to be.

J-30: Growing Into Your Wonderful Self

J-30: Prelude

As I shed the parts of myself that were of no benefit, I've grown to truly love the person I'm becoming. It feels good to embrace self-love. The way I speak, think, and view myself is constantly transforming for the better.

Title: Growing Into Your Wonderful Self

Introduction

• Main Idea: God created each person with unique gifts, a purpose, and a calling to reflect His glory. Growing into your wonderful self means embracing your identity in Christ, developing your gifts, and walking confidently in who God made you to be.

• Scripture Reference: Psalm 139:14 – "I praise You because I am fearfully and wonderfully made; Your works are wonderful, I know that full well."

• Purpose: To encourage believers to discover their God-given identity, embrace their uniqueness, and grow into the wonderful person God designed them to be.

Main Points
I. Embracing Your God-Given Identity

1. You Are Fearfully and Wonderfully Made:
• God intricately designed you with purpose and love.
  • Jeremiah 1:5 – "Before I formed you in the womb I knew you, before you were born I set you apart."

2. You Are a New Creation in Christ:
• Through salvation, your identity is rooted in Christ.
  • 2 Corinthians 5:17 – "Therefore, if anyone is in Christ, the new creation has come: The old has gone, the new is here!"

3. You Are Chosen and Loved by God:
• Embrace the truth of your belonging and worth.
  • Ephesians 1:4-5 – "For He chose us in Him before the creation of the world to be holy and blameless in His sight."

II. Developing Your Unique Gifts and Talents

1. Recognize Your God-Given Gifts:
- Every believer has been uniquely equipped for good works.
  - 1 Peter 4:10 – "Each of you should use whatever gift you have received to serve others, as faithful stewards of God's grace."

2. Steward Your Talents Well:
- Growth requires intentional use and development of your abilities.
  - Matthew 25:29 – "For whoever has will be given more, and they will have an abundance."

3. Be Confident in Your Calling:
- Trust God's plan for your life and step into it boldly.
  - Philippians 1:6 – "Being confident of this, that He who began a good work in you will carry it on to completion."

III. Overcoming Barriers to Growth

1. Let Go of Comparisons:
- Avoid comparing yourself to others; focus on your unique path.
  - Galatians 6:4 – "Each one should test their own actions. Then they can take pride in themselves alone, without comparing themselves to someone else."

2. Trust God Amid Uncertainty:
- Growth may feel uncomfortable, but God is guiding you.
  - Isaiah 41:10 – "Do not fear, for I am with you; do not be dismayed, for I am your God."

3. Break Free from Limiting Beliefs:
- Renew your mind and align your thoughts with God's truth.
  - Romans 12:2 – "Be transformed by the renewing of your mind."

IV. Living as Your Wonderful Self

1. Walk in Love and Grace:
• Reflect God's love in your actions and interactions.
  • Colossians 3:12 – "Therefore, as God's chosen people, holy and dearly loved, clothe yourselves with compassion, kindness, humility, gentleness, and patience."

2. Shine Your Light Boldly:
• Be a testimony of God's work in your life.
  • Matthew 5:16 – "Let your light shine before others, that they may see your good deeds and glorify your Father in heaven."

3. Grow Through Every Season:
• Trust God's process and timing for your growth.
  • Ecclesiastes 3:1 – "There is a time for everything, and a season for every activity under the heavens."

Application/Solutions

Steps to Grow Into Your Wonderful Self

1. Spend Time with God Daily:
• Prayer and Scripture reveal God's purpose for your life.
  • Psalm 119:105 – "Your word is a lamp for my feet, a light on my path."

2. Seek Godly Counsel and Community:
• Surround yourself with people who encourage your growth.
  • Proverbs 27:17 – "As iron sharpens iron, so one person sharpens another."

3. Celebrate Your Progress:
• Rejoice in the ways God is shaping and growing you.
  • 1 Thessalonians 5:18 – "Give thanks in all circumstances."

Conclusion

• Summary: Growing into your wonderful self is a journey of discovering your God-given identity, developing your unique gifts, and living boldly in God's purpose for your life.

• Encouragement: Trust that God has equipped you to fulfill your calling. Embrace your uniqueness and grow into the person He created you to be.

• Call to Action: As you embrace each day, commit to pursuing spiritual and personal growth. Step into the fullness of who you are in Christ.

Reflection Questions

1. What steps can you take to embrace your God-given identity?
2. How can you develop and use your gifts to glorify God?
3. What barriers are holding you back from fully growing into your wonderful self?

Resolve to grow into your wonderful self by seeking God's guidance, walking in His purpose, and reflecting His glory in every area of your life.

J-31: How Not to Become an Exhausting Person Unto God

J-31: Prelude

We, as a people, can be exhausting. Sometimes I imagine God saying, *"All you do is complain, gripe, and moan. No matter what I do, it's never enough. Some of you don't even realize the blessings you have right now. You want what you want, and you want it now. You're quick to blame Me for your downfalls when it's your choices that led you here."*

And what about those who pray and pray but lack true belief or faith? What must God think of that?

Title: How Not to Become an Exhausting Person Unto God

Introduction

- Emotionally Draining Person Defined: one who complains criticize, or express pessimism; a people who are surrounded by drama, constantly complaining, or are an emotional wreck.

- Main Idea: While God's patience is infinite, we must strive to live in a way that delights His heart rather than grieves His Spirit. By aligning our lives with His will and growing in faith, we honor His grace and avoid exhausting His loving patience.

- Scripture Reference: Ephesians 4:30 – "And do not grieve the Holy Spirit of God, with whom you were sealed for the day of redemption."

- Purpose: To encourage believers to live lives of faith, obedience, and gratitude, so they bring joy to God rather than burden His Spirit with disobedience, complaints, or lack of faith.

Main Points
I. Understand What Grieves God

1. Lack of Faith:
- Doubting God's promises or His ability to provide wears on His Spirit.
  - Hebrews 11:6 – "And without faith it is impossible to please God."

2. Disobedience to His Will:
- Ignoring His commandments or delaying obedience is exhausting to God's patience.
  - Jonah 1:3 – "But Jonah ran away from the Lord and headed for Tarshish."

3. Complaining and Grumbling:
- Constant complaints show a lack of trust and gratitude for His provision.
  - Philippians 2:14-15 – "Do everything without grumbling or arguing."

II. Live a Life That Pleases God

1. Trust in God Completely:
• Faith pleases God and brings Him joy.
  • Proverbs 3:5-6 – "Trust in the Lord with all your heart and lean not on your own understanding."

2. Obey His Commands:
• Joyful obedience shows love and respect for God's authority.
  • John 14:15 – "If you love me, keep my commands."

3. Be Grateful in All Things:
• Gratitude prevents complaints and honors God's blessings.
  • 1 Thessalonians 5:18 – "Give thanks in all circumstances; for this is God's will for you in Christ Jesus."

III. Cultivate a Heart That Delights God

1. Spend Time in His Presence:
• Prayer and worship draw you closer to God and align your heart with His.
  • Psalm 16:11 – "You make known to me the path of life; you will fill me with joy in your presence."

2. Bear Fruit of the Spirit:
• Living out love, joy, and peace reflects God's work in you.
• Galatians 5:22-23 – "The fruit of the Spirit is love, joy, peace, forbearance, kindness, goodness, faithfulness, gentleness, and self-control."

3. Encourage Others in Faith:
• Building up others in faith shows God's love and avoids selfish tendencies.
  • Hebrews 10:24 – "Let us consider how we may spur one another on toward love and good deeds."

Application/Solutions
Practical Steps to Avoid Being Exhausting to God

1. Reflect Daily on God's Goodness:
- Make gratitude a habit to counter complaints and doubts.
  - Psalm 103:2 – "Praise the Lord, my soul, and forget not all His benefits."

2. Seek Forgiveness and Repentance:
- Regularly examine your heart and turn away from sin.
  - 1 John 1:9 – "If we confess our sins, He is faithful and just and will forgive us our sins."

3. Stay Rooted in God's Word:
- Scripture provides guidance and strengthens your faith.
  - Psalm 119:11 – "I have hidden your word in my heart that I might not sin against you."

4. Practice Patience and Contentment:
- Trust God's timing and be content with His provision.
  - Philippians 4:11-12 – "I have learned the secret of being content in any and every situation."

Conclusion

- Summary: God is patient and loving, but He desires our faith, obedience, and gratitude. By living in alignment with His will, we avoid becoming spiritually exhausting and instead bring Him joy.

- Encouragement: God's grace empowers us to change our habits and grow into people who delight His heart.

- Call to Action: As you embrace each day, examine areas where you may be grieving God's Spirit. Commit to trust, obedience, and gratitude as a way to honor His love.

Reflection Questions

1. Are there areas in your life where you feel you may be grieving God's Spirit?
2. How can you grow in faith and obedience to reflect trust in God?
3. What practical steps will you take in the future to live in a way that delights God?

Resolve to live with faith, gratitude, and obedience to honor God's grace and avoid becoming exhausting to His Spirit. Let your life reflect His glory and bring joy to His heart.

J-32: Human Being vs. Human Doing

J-32: Prelude

Some things in life require deeper clarity and understanding. Gaining this insight has been a pivotal part of my journey.

Title: Human Being vs. Human Doing

Introduction

- Main Idea: God calls us to focus on who we are in Him—our identity as His children—rather than solely on what we do. While actions are important, they must flow from a heart centered on being in His presence.

- Scripture Reference: Psalm 46:10 – "Be still, and know that I am God."

- Purpose: To explore the difference between being a human "being"—rooted in our identity in Christ—and a human "doing," overly focused on accomplishments and works, and to learn how to balance both in God's will.

Main Points
I. Understanding the Difference

1. Human Being:
- Rooted in identity as God's child, prioritizing relationship with Him.
  - Genesis 1:27 – "So God created mankind in His own image."
  - Ephesians 2:10 – "For we are God's handiwork, created in Christ Jesus to do good works."

2. Human Doing:
- Focused on tasks, achievements, or pleasing others through works.
  - Matthew 7:22-23 – "Many will say to me on that day, 'Lord, Lord, did we not prophesy in your name?'...Then I will tell them plainly, 'I never knew you.'"

3. Balance Is Necessary:
- Doing flows from being; actions without identity in Christ become empty.
  - John 15:4 – "Remain in me, as I also remain in you. No branch can bear fruit by itself."

II. The Danger of Overemphasis on Doing

1. Burnout and Striving:
- When our focus is solely on doing, we lose sight of God's peace and grace.
  - Matthew 11:28-30 – "Come to me, all you who are weary and burdened, and I will give you rest."

2. Self-Reliance Over God-Reliance:
- Doing too much can shift focus from God's power to our own strength.
  - Proverbs 3:5-6 – "Trust in the Lord with all your heart and lean not on your own understanding."

3. Missed Relationship with God:
- Being busy for God can mean missing time with Him.
  - Luke 10:41-42 – "Martha, Martha…Mary has chosen what is better."

III. Embracing the Call to Be

1. Root Yourself in God's Presence:
- Spend time in prayer, Scripture, and stillness to cultivate your identity.
  - Isaiah 40:31 – "But those who hope in the Lord will renew their strength."

2. Know Your Worth Comes from God, Not Works:
- God loves us for who we are, not for what we do.
  - Romans 5:8 – "But God demonstrates His own love for us in this: While we were still sinners, Christ died for us."

3. Live Out of Overflow:
- Actions flow naturally when you're aligned with God's Spirit.
  - John 7:38 – "Whoever believes in me…rivers of living water will flow from within them."

Application/Solutions
Practical Steps to Balance Being and Doing

1. Start Each Day in Stillness:
• Begin with prayer and quiet reflection to center yourself in God.
  • Psalm 5:3 – "In the morning, Lord, you hear my voice; in the morning I lay my requests before you and wait expectantly."

2. Evaluate Your Motives:
• Ask whether your actions are driven by love for God or desire for recognition.
  • Colossians 3:23-24 – "Whatever you do, work at it with all your heart, as working for the Lord."

3. Schedule Time for Rest and Worship:
• Intentionally set aside moments to "be" with God, free from tasks.
  • Exodus 20:8-10 – "Remember the Sabbath day by keeping it holy."

4. Focus on Relationships, Not Just Results:
• Prioritize people and spiritual growth over achievements.
  • Philippians 2:3-4 – "Do nothing out of selfish ambition…value others above yourselves."

Conclusion

• Summary: Being rooted in Christ must come before doing for Christ. By embracing who we are in Him, our actions become meaningful and aligned with His will.

• Encouragement: As you embrace each day, let us commit to "being" in God's presence daily, trusting that He will guide our "doing."

• Call to Action: Reflect on your life: Are you striving in your own strength, or are you living out of an identity rooted in God? Take steps to reconnect with Him and rest in His love.

Reflection Questions
1. Do you prioritize being with God over doing for Him?
2. What are practical ways you can spend more time in God's presence?
3. How can your actions flow more naturally from your identity in Christ?

Resolve to focus on being a child of God first, allowing your actions to flow naturally from your relationship with Him. Let this year be one of rest, growth, and fruitful service rooted in His love.

J-33: Celebrate Self: Embracing Your God-Given Identity

J-33: Prelude

I've never been comfortable with people making a big deal about me. However, I've learned the importance of celebrating yourself. No one will celebrate you quite like you can. Celebrate both your successes and your failures—because failures are simply lessons learned. Whether your celebrations are big or small, take time to appreciate yourself. After all, who ever gets tired of being celebrated?

Title: Celebrate Self: Embracing Your God-Given Identity

Introduction

• Main Idea: Celebrating oneself is not about pride or self-centeredness but about honoring the person God created you to be. Embracing your unique identity glorifies God and allows you to serve His purpose joyfully.

• Scripture Reference: Psalm 139:14 – "I praise you because I am fearfully and wonderfully made; your works are wonderful, I know that full well."

• Purpose: To encourage believers to see themselves as God does and to celebrate their God-given identity, talents, and purpose with humility and gratitude.

Main Points

I. Recognizing Your Worth in God

1. Created in His Image:
• Each person reflects God's glory and creativity.
  • Genesis 1:27 – "So God created mankind in His own image, in the image of God He created them."

2. Uniquely Designed for a Purpose:
• God has crafted each individual with specific gifts and talents.
  • Jeremiah 1:5 – "Before I formed you in the womb, I knew you; before you were born, I set you apart."

3. Loved and Redeemed by Christ:
• Your worth is rooted in God's love and the sacrifice of Jesus.
  • Romans 5:8 – "But God demonstrates His own love for us in this: While we were still sinners, Christ died for us."

II. The Importance of Celebrating Self

1. Honoring God's Creation:
• Celebrating yourself honors the Creator who made you.
  • Isaiah 64:8 – "We are the clay, you are the potter; we are all the work of your hand."

2. Gratitude for Your Gifts:
• Recognizing your strengths and abilities fosters gratitude.
  • James 1:17 – "Every good and perfect gift is from above, coming down from the Father of the heavenly lights."

3. Strengthening Your Identity in Christ:
• Embracing who you are in Christ builds confidence to live out your purpose.
  • Ephesians 2:10 – "For we are God's handiwork, created in Christ Jesus to do good works."

III. Balancing Humility and Confidence

1. Celebrate with Humility:
• Acknowledge God as the source of your strengths.
  • 1 Corinthians 4:7 – "What do you have that you did not receive? And if you did receive it, why do you boast as though you did not?"

2. Avoid Comparison:
• Celebrate your uniqueness without comparing yourself to others.
  • Galatians 6:4-5 – "Each one should test their own actions. Then they can take pride in themselves alone, without comparing themselves to someone else."

3. Use Your Gifts for God's Glory:
• Celebration leads to stewardship; use your talents to serve others.
  • 1 Peter 4:10 – "Each of you should use whatever gift you have received to serve others."

Application/Solutions
Practical Ways to Celebrate Yourself in a Godly Manner

1. Practice Self-Reflection:
• Regularly acknowledge your growth and achievements in Christ.
  • Lamentations 3:22-23 – "His compassions never fail. They are new every morning; great is your faithfulness."

2. Speak Life Over Yourself:
• Replace negative self-talk with affirmations based on God's Word.
  • Proverbs 18:21 – "The tongue has the power of life and death."

3. Celebrate Your Milestones:
• Acknowledge your progress and give thanks to God.
  • Philippians 4:6 – "Do not be anxious about anything, but in every situation, by prayer and petition, with thanksgiving, present your requests to God."

4. Share Your Joy with Others:
• Let your celebration inspire and uplift those around you.
  • Matthew 5:16 – "Let your light shine before others, that they may see your good deeds and glorify your Father in heaven."

Conclusion

• Summary: Celebrating yourself is an act of worship when done with humility and gratitude to God. Recognize that your identity, talents, and purpose are gifts from Him to be cherished and used for His glory.

• Encouragement: As you embrace each day, reflect on the person God has made you to be. Celebrate the growth, achievements, and blessings He has brought into your life.

• Call to Action: Identify one aspect of yourself you may have overlooked or undervalued. Take time to thank God for it and commit to using it for His purposes.

Reflection Questions
1. How often do you thank God for who He has created you to be?
2. What are some specific talents or traits you can celebrate today?
3. How can you use your God-given gifts to bless others and glorify Him?

Celebrate yourself as God's creation. Embrace your unique identity in Christ, nurture your talents, and live confidently in the purpose He has given you.

J-34: Eliminating Habits & Vices of Sin

J-34: Prelude

We all have habits and vices. I'm not here to list mine or call out anyone else's. I simply ask: Is your habit or vice pleasing to God? Is it a reflection of Christ? Even if it seems harmless or personal, it could become a stronghold —and strongholds can be broken.

Title: Eliminating Habits & Vices of Sin

Introduction

• Main Idea: Breaking free from sinful habits and vices requires intentionality, reliance on God's power, and the discipline to walk in righteousness. God calls us to holiness and equips us through His Word and Spirit.

• Scripture Reference: Romans 6:12-14 – "Therefore do not let sin reign in your mortal body so that you obey its evil desires. Do not offer any part of yourself to sin as an instrument of wickedness, but rather offer yourselves to God as those who have been brought from death to life."

• Purpose: To equip believers with biblical principles and practical steps to overcome sin and live a life of righteousness and victory in Christ.

Main Points

I. Understanding Sin and Its Power

1. The Deceptive Nature of Sin:
• Sin appears pleasurable but leads to destruction.
 • James 1:14-15 – "Each person is tempted when they are dragged away by their own evil desire and enticed. Then, after desire has conceived, it gives birth to sin; and sin, when it is full-grown, gives birth to death."

2. The Battle Between Flesh and Spirit:
• Believers face a constant struggle between their sinful nature and their new life in Christ.
 • Galatians 5:16-17 – "So I say, walk by the Spirit, and you will not gratify the desires of the flesh."

3. The Consequences of Sin:
• Sin separates us from God and hinders our spiritual growth.
 • Isaiah 59:2 – "Your iniquities have separated you from your God; your sins have hidden His face from you."

II. The Call to Eliminate Sinful Habits

1. Repentance is the Starting Point:
- Genuine repentance involves turning away from sin and turning toward God.
  - Acts 3:19 – "Repent, then, and turn to God, so that your sins may be wiped out."

2. Rely on God's Strength:
- Victory over sin comes through the power of the Holy Spirit.
  - 2 Corinthians 12:9 – "My grace is sufficient for you, for my power is made perfect in weakness."

3. Renew Your Mind:
- Replace sinful thoughts with God's truth.
  - Romans 12:2 – "Do not conform to the pattern of this world, but be transformed by the renewing of your mind."

III. Practical Steps to Overcome Sin

1. Identify and Confess Sin:
- Acknowledge specific sins and bring them before God in prayer.
  - 1 John 1:9 – "If we confess our sins, He is faithful and just and will forgive us our sins and purify us from all unrighteousness."

2. Avoid Temptation:
- Take proactive steps to avoid situations that lead to sin.
  - 1 Corinthians 10:13 – "No temptation has overtaken you except what is common to mankind. And God is faithful; He will not let you be tempted beyond what you can bear."

3. Develop New Habits:
- Replace sinful behaviors with godly ones, such as prayer, Bible study, and serving others.
  - Colossians 3:5 – "Put to death, therefore, whatever belongs to your earthly nature."

4. Surround Yourself with Accountability:
- Seek the support of mature believers who will encourage and challenge you.
  - Proverbs 27:17 – "As iron sharpens iron, so one person sharpens another."

IV. Living in Freedom and Holiness

1. Walk by the Spirit:
- Depend on the Holy Spirit daily for guidance and strength.
  - Galatians 5:25 – "Since we live by the Spirit, let us keep in step with the Spirit."

2. Claim Your Identity in Christ:
- Remember you are no longer a slave to sin but a new creation.
  - 2 Corinthians 5:17 – "If anyone is in Christ, the new creation has come: The old has gone, the new is here!"

3. Celebrate Progress:
- Rejoice in small victories as you grow in holiness.
  - Philippians 1:6 – "He who began a good work in you will carry it on to completion."

Application/Solutions
Daily Practices for Victory Over Sin

1. Start Your Day in Prayer:
- Commit your day to God and ask for His guidance and strength.
  - Psalm 5:3 – "In the morning, Lord, you hear my voice; in the morning I lay my requests before you."

2. Meditate on God's Word:
- Fill your heart with Scripture to combat temptation.
  - Psalm 119:11 – "I have hidden your word in my heart that I might not sin against you."

3. Celebrate God's Grace:
• Focus on God's forgiveness and grace, which empowers you to change.
  • Hebrews 4:16 – "Let us then approach God's throne of grace with confidence."

Conclusion

• Summary: Eliminating sinful habits and vices is a process of surrendering to God, renewing your mind, and walking in the Spirit. Victory over sin is possible through Christ, who has already overcome the world.

• Encouragement: As you embrace each day, trust that God's grace is sufficient to help you break free from any sinful habit. His power is at work within you, transforming you into the person He created you to be.

• Call to Action: Identify one habit or vice you need to surrender to God. Commit to specific steps and ask for His help in walking in freedom and holiness.

Reflection Questions

1. What habits or vices are hindering your relationship with God?
2. How can you incorporate Scripture and prayer into your daily life to combat sin?
3. Who can you rely on for accountability and encouragement in your journey to holiness?

Commit to walking in holiness by relying on God's strength, renewing your mind, and eliminating habits and vices that hinder your spiritual growth. Trust in His grace to sustain and transform you.

J-35: Jesus: The Way, The Truth, The Messenger

J-35: Prelude

I'm just going to say His name: Jesus.

Title: Jesus: The Way, The Truth, The Messenger

Introduction

- Main Idea: Jesus Christ embodies the path to salvation, reveals ultimate truth, and serves as the divine Messenger who bridges humanity to God. His life and teachings provide the blueprint for eternal life, spiritual clarity, and reconciliation with God.

- Scripture Reference: John 14:6 – "Jesus answered, 'I am the way and the truth and the life. No one comes to the Father except through me.'"

- Purpose: To explore the role of Jesus as the Way to salvation, the Truth in a world of confusion, and the Messenger of God's love and grace.

Main Points
I. Jesus: The Way

1. The Way to the Father:
- Jesus is the only path to God, offering salvation through His sacrifice.
  - Acts 4:12 – "Salvation is found in no one else, for there is no other name under heaven given to mankind by which we must be saved."

2. The Way of Righteousness:
- Jesus calls us to walk in obedience and follow His example.
  - Matthew 7:13-14 – "Enter through the narrow gate. For wide is the gate and broad is the road that leads to destruction, and many enter through it. But small is the gate and narrow the road that leads to life."

3. The Way to Eternal Life:
- Through His death and resurrection, Jesus secures eternal life for believers.
  - John 11:25-26 – "I am the resurrection and the life. The one who believes in me will live, even though they die."

II. Jesus: The Truth

1. Truth in His Word:
- Jesus' teachings reveal God's will and bring clarity in a world of falsehoods.
  - John 17:17 – "Sanctify them by the truth; your word is truth."

2. Truth About God's Character:
- Jesus perfectly reflects God's love, mercy, and justice.
  - Colossians 1:15 – "The Son is the image of the invisible God, the firstborn over all creation."

3. Truth That Sets Us Free:
- Believing in Jesus liberates us from sin and spiritual bondage.
  - John 8:32 – "Then you will know the truth, and the truth will set you free."

III. Jesus: The Messenger

1. Messenger of Reconciliation:
- Jesus bridges the gap between humanity and God, offering peace and forgiveness.
  - 2 Corinthians 5:18-19 – "All this is from God, who reconciled us to himself through Christ and gave us the ministry of reconciliation."

2. Messenger of God's Kingdom:
- Jesus proclaimed the coming of God's Kingdom and invited all to partake in it.
  - Matthew 4:17 – "Repent, for the kingdom of heaven has come near."

3. Messenger of Eternal Hope:
- Jesus delivers the promise of eternal life and hope for the future.
  - John 10:10 – "I have come that they may have life, and have it to the full."

Application/Solutions
Living Out Jesus as The Way, The Truth, and The Messenger

1. Follow His Path:
- Commit to walking in obedience and imitating Christ's example.
  - 1 John 2:6 – "Whoever claims to live in him must live as Jesus did."

2. Hold Fast to His Truth:
- Study and meditate on His Word to align your life with God's will.
  - Psalm 119:105 – "Your word is a lamp for my feet, a light on my path."

3. Share His Message:
- Be an ambassador of Christ by sharing His love and hope with others.
  - Matthew 28:19-20 – "Therefore go and make disciples of all nations."

Conclusion

- Summary: Jesus is the Way to salvation, the Truth that brings freedom, and the Messenger who delivers God's love and grace. Embracing Him transforms our lives and equips us to live with purpose and hope.

- Encouragement: As you embrace each day, let us fix our eyes on Jesus, walking in His way, standing firm in His truth, and sharing His message with a world in need.

- Call to Action: Reflect on how you can deepen your relationship with Jesus and embody His teachings in your daily life.

Reflection Questions

1. In what areas of your life do you need to follow Jesus' way more closely?
2. How can you grow in your understanding of Jesus as the Truth?
3. Who in your life needs to hear the message of hope found in Jesus?

Commit to embracing Jesus as the Way, the Truth, and the Messenger by following His example, standing firm in His Word, and sharing His message with others.

J-36: Journey of Reading God's Word: Walking in Truth & Growth

J-36: Prelude

I began journaling my transformation on January 1, 2024, without any idea that it would lead to writing this book. On December 5, God spoke to me and said, *"Share what you've written."* I responded, "Huh? Do what again?" But God repeated, *"Share."*

Remembering the consequences of disobedience and the blessings of obedience, I chose the latter. I pray that my journey resonates with you and that it blesses you as much as it has blessed me.

~Blessings 🖤

Title: Journey of Reading God's Word: Walking in Truth & Growth

Introduction

• Main Idea: The Word of God is our roadmap for life. Embarking on a journey of reading and meditating on Scripture transforms our minds, nourishes our souls, and equips us to live in obedience to God's will.

• Scripture Reference: Psalm 119:105 – "Your word is a lamp for my feet, a light on my path."

• Purpose: To inspire believers to prioritize reading, understanding, and applying God's Word as a daily habit each day, leading to spiritual growth and deeper intimacy with God.

Main Points

I. The Importance of God's Word

1. The Word as Divine Revelation:
• The Bible reveals God's character, promises, and plan for humanity.
  • 2 Timothy 3:16-17 – "All Scripture is God-breathed and is useful for teaching, rebuking, correcting, and training in righteousness, so that the servant of God may be thoroughly equipped for every good work."

2. The Word Brings Spiritual Growth:
• Reading Scripture strengthens our faith and aligns us with God's purposes.
  • Romans 10:17 – "Faith comes by hearing, and hearing by the word of God."

II. The Benefits of Reading God's Word

1. Transformation of Mind and Heart:
• Scripture renews our thinking and shapes our character.
  • Romans 12:2 – "Do not conform to the pattern of this world, but be transformed by the renewing of your mind."

2. Guidance for Daily Living:
• God's Word provides wisdom and direction.
  • Proverbs 3:5-6 – "Trust in the Lord with all your heart and lean not on your own understanding; in all your ways submit to Him, and He will make your paths straight."

3. Spiritual Protection:
• The Word is our weapon against temptation and spiritual attacks.
  • Ephesians 6:17 – "Take the helmet of salvation and the sword of the Spirit, which is the word of God."

III. Overcoming Challenges in the Journey

1. Distractions and Busyness:
• Prioritize time with God above daily obligations.
  • Matthew 6:33 – "Seek first His kingdom and His righteousness, and all these things will be given to you as well."

2. Understanding Difficult Passages:
• Seek the Holy Spirit's guidance for understanding Scripture.
  • John 14:26 – "The Holy Spirit… will teach you all things and will remind you of everything I have said to you."

3. Spiritual Dryness:
• Persist in reading, trusting God to rekindle your passion for His Word.
  • Isaiah 40:31 – "Those who hope in the Lord will renew their strength."

IV. Practical Steps for a Fruitful Journey

1. Set a Reading Plan:
• Commit to reading the Bible daily through a structured plan.
  • Psalm 1:2 – "But whose delight is in the law of the Lord, and who meditates on His law day and night."

2. Meditate and Memorize Scripture:
- Reflect deeply on the verses you read and commit key passages to memory.
  - Joshua 1:8 – "Keep this Book of the Law always on your lips; meditate on it day and night."

3. Apply the Word to Your Life:
- Let Scripture guide your actions and decisions.
  - James 1:22 – "Do not merely listen to the word... Do what it says."

4. Join a Community for Accountability:
- Share your journey with others for encouragement and growth.
  - Hebrews 10:24-25 – "Let us consider how we may spur one another on toward love and good deeds, not giving up meeting together."

Application/Solutions
Living Out the Journey:

1. Start Small but Be Consistent:
- Begin with a chapter or passage daily, gradually building your habit.

2. Create a Quiet Space for Study:
- Dedicate a distraction-free environment for your time with God.

3. Pray for Insight and Guidance:
- Begin each session by asking the Holy Spirit to illuminate God's truth.

4. Keep a Journal:
- Record your reflections, prayers, and lessons learned from Scripture.

Conclusion

- Summary: Reading God's Word is a journey of transformation that leads to wisdom, strength, and intimacy with God.

• Encouragement: As you embrace each day, commit to walking daily with God through His Word, trusting that He will reveal Himself to you and guide your steps.

• Call to Action: Colossians 3:16 – "Let the message of Christ dwell among you richly." Let this year be the year you deeply root yourself in Scripture and see the fruit of God's Word in your life.

Reflection Questions
1. What is one step you can take today to start or deepen your journey of reading God's Word?
2. How has the Bible shaped your understanding of God and yourself?
3. Who can you encourage to join you in a commitment to Scripture this day, this year?

May the journey of reading God's Word this day, this year bring you closer to Him and transform every aspect of your life!

Closing Scripture

2 Corinthians 12:5-10, 14

5 Examine yourselves to see whether you are in the faith; test yourselves. Do you not realize that Christ Jesus is in you—unless, of course, you fail the test? 6 And I trust that you will discover that we have not failed the test. 7 Now we pray to God that you will not do anything wrong—not so that people will see that we have stood the test but so that you will do what is right even though we may seem to have failed. 8 For we cannot do anything against the truth, but only for the truth. 9 We are glad whenever we are weak but you are strong; and our prayer is that you may be fully restored. 10 This is why I write these things when I am absent, that when I come I may not have to be harsh in my use of authority—the authority the Lord gave me for building you up, not for tearing you down.

14 May the grace of the Lord Jesus Christ, and the love of God, and the fellowship of the Holy Spirit be with you all.

Amen.

www.ingramcontent.com/pod-product-compliance
Lightning Source LLC
Chambersburg PA
CBHW070424010526
44118CB00014B/1897